BEING
BLACK

REDISCOVERING A LOST IDENTITY

ZIRI DAFRANCHI

A Trilogy of Truth Collection

HEREDITAS
PRESS
For truth and freedom

Hereditas Press
www.hereditaspress.com

For the "lost" Israelites...that they may rediscover themselves.

IDENTITY AND DESTINY

Identity and destiny are entwined; identity is predetermined by destiny, while destiny is dependent on identity for its realisation.

A people without the right identity are a people derailed from their rightful destiny because a wrong identity could never result in the right destiny.

Destiny is the reason a people are a people, but to fulfil it, the people must first rediscover their lost identity.

.

Contents

Preface

Black is one of the two most common racial categories of humans today, the other is White. The world today is one where humans are classified into different racial groups mostly based on skin colour (e.g., Black, White), and in some cases on geography (e.g., African, Asian). In the USA, for instance, a person is regarded either as an American Indian or Alaska Native, Asian, Black or African American, Hispanic or Latino, Native Hawaiian or Other Pacific Islander, or White. In the UK, where the term ethnicity is used in preference to race, a person is formally identified either as White, Mixed, Asian or Asian British, Black or African or Caribbean or Black British, Arab, or any other specified group. You would have easily and quickly noticed the subjective nature of the criteria used for these classifications—while some classifications are based on geography, others are based on skin colour. Also, curiously, while a person can be an American Indian or African American in the USA, or African, Caribbean, or Black British in the UK, a person is simply White in both the USA and UK and not European

American or European British, for instance. Thus underlining the subjective as well as the biased nature of these racial classification models, which nonetheless remain the official means of categorising people in the referenced countries.
Similarly flawed models of racial classification are in use in different continents of the world. Consequently, this concept of racial grouping, although largely flawed, is one generally and strongly upheld by most people if not everyone in today's world. A person regardless of age, gender, or academic qualification, would easily self-identify or be identified as White or Black, in most cases, usually, simply based on skin colour. Interestingly, humans have not always been divided into racial categories, at least not until much later in our collective history. I had been completely ignorant of this fact until I started researching this book and I believe there are many more people like myself who despite their academic achievements remain in the dark as to the truth about the racial categorisation of humans.

Race, as a categorising term in reference to humans, came into use in the English language late in the sixteenth century, from the Old French *rasse* (1512), from Italian *razza*, originally interpreted to mean an identifiable group of people who share a common descent. By the eighteenth century, the meaning and use of the term "race" had evolved, subsequently becoming a social tool for sorting and ranking the peoples in the English colonies particularly in today's USA—i.e., Europeans who saw themselves as free people, Amerindians who had been conquered, and Africans who were being brought in as slave labour. Sadly, this usage continues today. It is instructive to note that the concept of race, starting from the eighteenth century, became reduced to nothing more than a social construct which was subsequently politicised and used to entitle the group of people who invented it—Europeans—at the expense of the other groups. Although several past and present efforts have been made by some scholars, starting from around the seventeenth century, to represent race as a scientific concept, none has yet been able to gain unquestionable credibility or acceptance. On the contrary, based on modern scholarship using highly advanced technology, there is a consensus among scholars that race lacks scientific credibility but instead is a social concept. For instance, what the Human Genome Project (HGP) determined was that there is the same amount of genetic variation among individuals within a so-called racial group as there is between individuals in different racial groups. The simple implication here is that there are no real genetic differences between the people now regarded as black and their white counterparts (i.e., based on modern racial classification models), or between whites and Asians, or between any of the so-called races. Putting it succinctly, nobody is Black and nobody is White either—we are all simply humans!

You may then wonder if this is the case, why I still chose to use the term "Black" in the title of this book: My use of Black in this book's title and narrative is purely based on contemporary usage—even though flawed—and primarily for ease of communication. I reasoned that it would be easier for me and for you the reader if I used the term "Black" or "White" in reference to particular groups of humans as opposed to sticking to a more scientifically accurate terminology, such as African, European, Asian, American, etc., because of the confusion likely to arise as a result. If I referred to American, for instance, then I would still have to qualify the particular American population group with either African-American or White-American. Furthermore,

Black and White are both used to represent population groups that cut across different geographical regions and thus using such terms as Black and White make it easier to discuss those groups collectively. It is important pointing out now that although the title Being Black suggests a totality, the main subjects of this book represent only a fraction of the overall global black population, although the plights discussed in this book affect blacks generally.

Although the African origin of humans is relatively common knowledge, especially among students of Anthropology, not many people outside the academia are aware of this. Personally, I was again ignorant in this regard until sometime in 2012 when I came across an online article by the BBC which highlighted the origin of humans in today's Africa. I have to confess, perhaps to my shame, that I was quite surprised by this realisation because until then, I never would have imagined Africa as the land of human origin, or even that humans all had a single origin. I believe there are even more people who are currently still in the dark regarding both our single and African origin. This situation is more down to miseducation than personal ignorance because almost everything we know about human history were things we learnt through the process of formal education. My ignorance and that of many others regarding human origins is, therefore, an indictment on our formal educational system which, for whatever reason, has relegated such studies to specialised disciplines taught at higher academic levels. Such studies ought to be taught starting from very early in childhood because human origins should form part of our primary knowledge. It is a vital necessity to know about our collective origin from very early in life because such knowledge would certainly benefit us by equipping us with the right mindsets among others. But then again, it is most likely that the exclusion of the study of human origins from early learning is intentional. Perhaps we were not even meant to know the truth about human origins so that the unhealthy status quo is maintained. Hence, such studies have been specialised and made exclusively available only to those who desire to pursue them.

Thanks to those among us who decided to study human origins, the rest of us are now privy to their research efforts and, as a result, we now know more about our foremost beginnings starting with our foremost ancestors. Although anthropological studies started with basic research methods and skills, significant advancements have been made in research techniques over several centuries, resulting in modern methods.

Modern scholarship has now shown that humans originated in today's Africa and with the skin colour known today as black. In today's parlance, our original human ancestors started life as "African Black." Prehistoric and historic migrations resulted in local or indigenous black populations in every of today's continents, as our ancestors began exploring the world. However, the original population of Africa did not remain intact till date but instead had also been greatly influenced by inward and outward migrations at different prehistoric and historic periods, sometimes from one part of the continent to another, meaning that a significant proportion of the current black populations in different parts of Africa are descendants of migrants.

A particular group of these "Black Africans"—some of whom were forcefully migrated out of the continent during historic slavery into Europe, the Americas, and the Caribbean—form the primary subject of this book. Due to continuous migration and assimilation, most people today are genuinely unaware of their original ethnic identity or heritage. A situation that incidentally, applies to the current population of black Africans who happen to be the subject of this book.

Another very important fact relevant to the objective of this book relates to geography. The region now classified as Africa is a reduced version of the original continent, which included a vast part of what is now known as the Middle East. The term "Middle East" is a political construct that came into existence very early in the twentieth century, becoming popularised after World War I. The term was coined in 1901 by US Admiral Alfred Thayer Mahan and was popularised in speeches in 1916 by British Parliamentarian Sir Mark Sykes. Prior to this invention, parts of the Middle East were originally classified under the African or Asian continent depending on the continental landmass they were part of. Consequently, places such as today's Yemen, Saudi Arabia, Israel, and Jordan were originally regarded as part of Africa's North East. It is instructive to note that the arbitrary grouping of places that rightly and ordinarily are part of Africa and Asia into the bogus concept called the Middle East was done by Europeans and for political reasons, as was the case with the concept of race.

My personal experience which culminated in the writing of *Being Black: Rediscovering A Lost Identity* began early in

2015, after what I can only describe as a spiritual awakening. It all started when I suddenly had an inexplicable urge to investigate my origins. Which ordinarily did not make any sense to me because at the time I had no doubts about my ethnicity or ancestry: I had always known I was Igbo—an ethnic group in South Eastern Nigeria—and could trace my family tree up to my paternal and maternal grandparents, at least, both of which had sufficed me. It started with my reflecting on the collective plights of a majority of black people all over the world, particularly those of relatively recent African descent. From the present systemic inequality, institutionalised racism, state-backed marginalisation and discrimination, and neo-colonialism, to past instances of historic colonisation and slavery, it immediately dawned on me that something was definitely wrong with this group of black people.

Two books that I came across at a local library presented me with a clearer picture of the past and ongoing tribulation of this breed of black people—Solomon Northup's *Twelve Years A Slave* and Wangari Maathai's *The Challenge For Africa*. The first book brought transatlantic slavery to life for me, which previously had largely been historical non-fiction, while the second book painted a graphic and gory picture of the current struggles of the African people in their fight to gain significant control of the natural resources they have been blessed with, which till then I only had a cursory knowledge of. I did read a few other books relating to the African people and their struggles.

I was so troubled that I wrote a two-part blog post titled Being Black and shared on social media, notably Google+ and Facebook. Although many people commented on the two posts, a particular comment by a lady in my Google+ circle left me bemused; she had ascribed what I then referred to as "The Black Problem" to the biblical curses placed on the people of ancient Israel—the descendants of Abraham through Isaac and Jacob. Largely due to my ignorance then, I couldn't agree with this viewpoint which I questioned rigorously. However, later in the same year (2015), I would dawn on my Hebraic roots, particularly Israelite. Again, through what can best be described as a supernatural experience. Although my people, Ndi Igbo, have often been associated with "Jews," a modern substitute for Israelites, howbeit incorrectly, I was never one of those who took this association seriously nor did I care. It was while watching a documentary on YouTube about the origin of the Igbo people that I became fully convinced that the association of the Igbo people with ancient Israelites had a credible basis. The biblical and historical evidence presented in the documentary was quite compelling.

A few years later, as I wrote and talked about Black Hebrews, I would discover that there are several other ethnic groups in parts of Africa, particularly West and Central, whom through research have been shown to have descended from ancient Israelite ancestors—e.g., the Akan people in today's Ghana and the Lemba people of Southern Africa. I also came across several research-based resources detailing the Hebrew ancestry of some ethnic groups in ancient Africa including, and notably, *From Babylon to Timbuktu: A History of the Ancient Black Races Including the Black Hebrews* by Rudolph R. Windsor.

Although by June 2019 I had written nothing less than three different drafts of this book under different subtitles, all based on extensive research, I was nonetheless not entirely satisfied with their contents, including that of the latest version completed late in May 2019. I was thus forced to take a long break from this project starting in June 2019 during which I was able to further my research in this regard. A major breakthrough came when I was brought in contact with some people who are part of the Hebrew Roots Movement; an ethnic and religious movement centred around the true identity of ancient Israelite descendants and a return to the Torah or the Laws given through biblical Moses to the ancient Israelites under the Abrahamic Covenant. This encounter proved very useful both on a personal and research bases because it afforded me with a wealth of resources through which I was deeply informed and better satisfied, intellectually and spiritually. Consequently, I was able to return to this project after over a year of withdrawal, this time, better equipped and thoroughly satisfied.

A greater part of the people this book is about are presently unaware it is about them, simply because they are still innocently unaware of their original and true ancestral identity and heritage, just as I had been before 2015.

Being Black: Rediscovering A Lost Identity is therefore written primarily so that every person today whose original ancestry is rightly traceable to the ancient Israelites would be awakened to this realisation. This is particularly important and relevant because of the promise of Israel's restoration in Isaiah 11:11–12, which is yet to be fulfilled but eventually will be fulfilled, thus: *And it shall come to pass in that day, That the Lord will set His hand again the second time To recover the remnant of His people,*

That shall remain from Assyria, and from Egypt, And from Pathros, and from Cush, and from Elam, And from Shinar, and from Hamath, and from the islands of the sea. And He will set up an ensign for the nations, And will assemble the dispersed of Israel, And gather together the scattered of Judah From the four corners of the earth (JPS Tanakh 1917).

I reason that before this restoration, and for its fulfilment, the people to be gathered would have to know who they originally and truly are because, as I also believe, they too would have a conscious role to play in their restoration. This book has also been written for the purpose of retelling an otherwise inaccurate rendition of history, particularly the history of the people who form its core subject and also that of Africa and her peoples at large. It is about time this wrong which has spanned millennia is righted and the world is made to know the true heritage of Africa and her various peoples as well as the true identity and heritage of ancient Israelites. It is now time for hidden truths to be uncovered and laid bare so that peace and justice may prevail and reign.

This book is not driven by emotions but rather credible evidence, it is not an adventurous experiment but rather a visionary prognosis of what is yet to come. Also, if this book comes across as somewhat controversial, kindly note it is so only because of the conspiracy of deception which has ensured that the truth it now reveals remained hidden and unpopular for more than a
millennium.

As no single work spanning so large a historical period, with its subject scattered across the globe, can hope to be comprehensive and minutely detailed, I do hope that the summarised narrative provided in relation to various relevant aspects of the subject would be sufficient in delivering the main objectives of the book and also that the bibliography would direct the reader to other resources for further reading and research. Considering that a bulk of my research for this book was of a secondary nature, I am indebted to the works, insights, and research of those before me from whom I have benefited. I am also grateful to my wonderful editor, Ujunwa Ogbonna, and other staff of Hereditas Press for their assistance. Lastly, I acknowledge my friends David Kasule and Jake Obichere for their unflinching support throughout the *Trilogy of Truth* project.

Being Black: Rediscovering A Lost Identity is the second book in my *Trilogy of Truth* (or *The Dafranchi Trilogy*), so captioned because of the truth-based nature of each book in the trilogy, and a trilogy because all three books are somewhat related and connected. Completing the trilogy are *Life: A Mystery Solved* and *Pagan World: Deception and Falsehood in Religion*.

CHAPTER ONE

Origins

Humanity has a single origin. A simple but also almost incredible fact considering the vast array of morphological differences observable in people from different parts of the world. Although the body plan is similar for all humans regardless of ethnicity or indigenous location, a closer examination of our physical characteristics would reveal a range of differences between and within broad population groups. For instance, there is a great range of skin colours, hair colours and textures, facial features, body sizes, and other physical traits in the local populations of each of today's continents as there are between continents. Using the contemporary racial classification of Black and White to illustrate: The skin colours of the two groups are noticeably different—one group has a darker shade while the other a lighter shade—but within each group, differences also exist in the degree of darkness and lightness. There are various shades of the dark skin colour as there are of the lighter variation. Similar differences abound with hair colours and textures. Some white people have natural blonde, brunette, ginger, black, auburn, and other hair colours while amongst black people, there are those with natural black, brown, auburn, and other shades of hair colours. With respect to hair textures, black people exhibit a mixture that includes curly, crinkly, wavy, kinky, or straight hair almost as much as white people also do, howbeit uniquely, which means that curls or waves, for instance, differ between the two groups. Black people are also generally known to have broad and flat noses, which are contrasted by the small and pointed noses of White people. There is a plethora of physical differences between and within the broad population groups commonly referred to as Black and White as there are between each of these groups and the other main population groups, or races, so much so that the idea of a single and common origin of humans might sound farfetched to some people.

Interestingly, these anatomical differences formed the basis of many studies carried out in anthropology and other fields, starting from as far back as the eighteenth century, to determine whether or not humans have a single origin. Needless pointing out that scholars have remained divided in their opinions in this regard while further studies are ongoing. There is, however, a consensus in anthropology that the primary ancestors of humans (scientifically, *Homo* species) originated in Africa! Note that Charles Darwin's theory of biological evolution is the basis of scientific studies of the origin of humans, and it argues that humans are a result of an evolutionary process. Based on this, humans, known scientifically to belong to the *Homo* species, are categorised into various *Homo* groups based on their evolutionary trend. *Homo habilis* ("handy man") is believed to be the earliest documented representative of the genus *Homo*, having "evolved around 2.8 million years ago," while *Homo sapiens* ("wise man"), representing the latest version of *Homo*, is believed to have "emerged in Africa around 300,000 years ago." Therefore, the consensus in anthropology is that the *Homo* species, the foremost ancestors of humans, originated in Africa.

The divided opinions fall into two main groups: those who argue that all of today's humans (or modern humans) descended from African ancestors and others who argue that modern humans descended independently from ancestors in different parts of the world. The first school of thought is known as the Out of Africa model (OOA), and the second is the Regional, or Multiregional, Continuity model. It is instructive to note that the Out of Africa model was the first to be upheld by scholars, and generally too, from the inception of anthropological studies during the eighteenth century, and it prevailed as a consensual theory till after World War II when pervasive racial bias began to influence scientific studies. It was not until 1984 that the Multiregional hypothesis was proposed, with paleoanthropologist Milford Howell Wolpoff as its leading proponent. Without delving deeply into scientific dialogue, the weight of research evidence lies highly in favour of the single African origin theory to the extent that there is now a new and additional model—the Recent African Origin model (ROA)— based on more recent research evidence. Before outlining some key research findings demonstrating a single African origin of humans, we shall first consider the very simple yet detailed account of how humans came into existence.

The Creation Story

The Hebrew Bible (also *Torah*, *Tanakh*, or the Old Testament Bible) presents an authoritative account of how humans and the entire universe came into existence. The key to unravelling existence is provided in the first verse of the first chapter of the first book, Genesis thus: *In the beginning God created the heaven and the earth.* This implies that the universe is not a product of a random happenstance but a deliberate plan and action by an identified supernatural being or entity—God (Hebrew, *Elohim*).

Light was the first thing to be created followed by the heavens; the earth; every species of plants that grow on land; sun, moon, and stars; all species of marine creatures and airborne birds; and then all species of animals. Finally, God decided to create Man (a generic term for humankind) thus: *And God said, Let us make man in our image, after our likeness: and let them have dominion over the fish of the sea, and over the fowl of the air, and over the cattle, and over all the earth, and over every creeping thing that creepeth upon the earth. So God created man in his own image, in the image of God created he him;* **male and female** *created he them. And God blessed them, and God said unto them,* **Be fruitful, and multiply, and replenish the earth**, *and sub-due it: and have dominion over the fish of the sea, and over the fowl of the air, and over every living thing that moveth upon the earth. And God said, Behold, I have given you every herb bearing seed, which is upon the face of all the earth, and every tree, in the* *which is the fruit of a tree yielding seed; to you it shall be for meat. And to every beast of the earth, and to every fowl of the air, and to every thing that creepeth upon the earth, wherein there is life, I have given every green herb for meat: and it was so.* (Genesis 1: 26–30. KJV).

The foregoing should suffice in explaining how humans and everything else created came about. Its simplicity could perhaps be why some scholars tend to reject it, opting instead for a more sophisticated scientific theory. Nonetheless, it is what it is, and it is impossible to reinvent the wheel. Hence, scientific theories put forward to explain how the universe came into existence have proved unsatisfactory, at the least. The origin of the universe, however, is not the subject matter here, rather, the human origin. The creation story supports a single human origin—in the first male and female created—who were empowered to multiply and replenish the earth. The entirety of humanity descended from that first male and female.

Although the creation story does not specifically name Africa as the land of origins—the Book of Genesis predates the name "Africa" anyway—some details in the second chapter of Genesis relating to the Garden of Eden, where God placed Man after creation, reveal Africa as the place where humans originated. The following provides identifiable markers for Eden's location: *And the LORD God planted a garden eastward in **Eden**; and there he put the man whom he had formed. And out of the ground made the LORD God to grow every tree that is pleasant to the sight, and good for food; the tree of life also in the midst of the garden, and the tree of knowledge of good and evil. And a river went out of Eden to water the garden; and from thence it was parted, and became into four heads. The name of* *the first is **Pison**: that is it which compasseth the whole land of **Hav'ilah**, where there is gold; and the gold of that land is good: there is bdellium and the onyx stone. And the name of the second river is **Gihon**: the same is it that compasseth the whole land of **Ethiopia**. And the name of the third river is **Hid'dekel**: that is it which goeth toward the east of **Assyria**. And the fourth river is **Euphra'tes**.* (Genesis 2: 8–14. KJV).

Due to changes over time in the names of places and rivers, locating Eden based on current geography is not as easy as it should have ordinarily been. For instance, the Ethiopia of today is a country in the Horn of Africa, but in times past, it was the name given to a vast region in Africa. In antiquity, ancient Greek historians such as Herodotus used the Greek equivalent of the word Ethiopia (Αἰθιοπία) to refer to the dwellers in the area immediate to the south of ancient Egypt, particularly areas under the ancient Kingdom of Kush, which comprise modern-day Nubia in Egypt and Sudan, and the entirety of Sub-Saharan Africa. Assyria no longer exists in name, although sizeable Assyrian populations remain in today's Syria. The Assyrian Empire existed in the area known today as the Levant, in eastern Mediterranean, encompassing an area which included all of Syria and more. The names of the rivers mentioned in the text have also changed over time, except for Euphra'tes. Nonetheless, using the known locations of the then Ethiopia (Africa) and Assyria (Eastern Mediterranean), it is reasonable pinning Eden in an area located within a region encompassing parts of Africa and eastern Mediterranean (a part of the Middle East, some regions which had been noted as being part of Africa originally).

Another biblical evidence supporting a single human origin is found in the story of the flood, during which the then world was destroyed except for a man named Noah, his wife, three sons and their wives, and a selection of all animal species.

Relevant details are recorded in the Bible as follows: *And the LORD said unto Noah, Come thou and all thy house into the ark; for thee have I seen righteous before me in this generation. Of every clean beast thou shalt take to thee by sevens, the male and his female: and of beasts that are not clean by two, the male and his female. Of fowls also of the air by sevens, the male and the female; to keep seed alive upon the face of all the earth. For yet seven days, and I will cause it to rain upon the earth forty days and forty nights; and every living substance that I have made will I destroy from off the face of the earth. And Noah did according unto all that the LORD commanded him. And Noah was six hundred years old when the flood of waters was upon the earth. And Noah went in, and his sons, and his wife, and his sons' wives with him, into the ark, because of the waters of the flood. Of clean beasts, and of beasts that are not clean, and of fowls, and of every thing that creepeth upon the earth, there went in two and two unto Noah into the ark, the male and the female, as God had commanded Noah. And it came to pass after seven days, that the waters of the flood were upon the earth. In the six hundredth year of Noah's life, in the second month, the seventeenth day of the month, the same day were all the fountains of the great deep broken up, and the windows of heaven were opened. And the rain was upon the earth forty days and forty nights. In the selfsame day entered Noah, and Shem, and Ham, and Japheth, the sons of Noah, and Noah's wife, and the three wives of his sons with them, into the ark; they, and every beast after his kind, and all the cattle after their kind, and every creeping thing that creepeth upon the earth after his kind, and every fowl after his kind, every bird of every sort. And they went in unto Noah into the ark, two and two of all flesh, wherein is the breath of life. And they that went in, went in male and female of all flesh, as God had commanded him: and the LORD shut him in. And the flood was forty days upon the earth; and the waters increased, and bare up the ark, and it was lifted up above the earth. And the waters prevailed, and were increased greatly upon the earth; and the ark went upon the face of the waters. And the waters prevailed exceedingly upon the earth; and all the high hills, that were under the whole heaven, were covered. Fifteen cubits upward did the waters prevail; and the mountains were covered. And all flesh died that moved upon the earth, both of fowl, and of cattle, and of beast, and of every creeping thing that creepeth upon the earth, and every man: all in whose nostrils was the breath of life, of all that was in the dry land, died. And every living substance was destroyed which was upon the face of the ground, both man, and cattle, and the creeping things, and the fowl of the heaven; and they were destroyed from the earth: and Noah only remained alive, and they that were with him in the ark. And the waters prevailed upon the earth a hundred and fifty days.* (Genesis 7 KJV).

A clear deduction from the foregoing is that no other human survived the flood apart from Noah and his household, which means every human born after the flood descended from Noah through his three sons—single-origin. An in-depth study of the biblical Book of Genesis reveals that after the first man and woman were expelled from the Garden of Eden (Genesis 3: 23–24) until humanity was scattered from their then location (Genesis 11: 1–8), human settlements were relatively localised, existing within proximity. The specific place where Noah would have lived is not recorded, but the Ark settled upon the mountains of Ar'arat (today's Ararat is in Turkey) after the flood, suggesting a near African location. Noah's descendants were scattered from a region, Shinar, for attempting to construct a tower in a city in the region known as Babel: Shinar is the southern region of Mesopotamia in today's Middle East, thus also indicating a near African location for humanity before being scattered across the globe.

Personally, I uphold the biblical account of creation and thus the origin of humans, not because of its simplicity but because I believe it to be true. Scientific evidence, incidentally, tends also to corroborate evidence from the creation story relating to a single human origin. We shall now explore some key research findings from different periods relating to human origins.

Evidence from Anthropology

The study of the origin and history of the human species is a relatively young science. It can be divided into two broad periods: The first began close to the eighteenth century lasting until the end of World War II (1945). From the beginning of the fifteenth century, explorers from Europe embarked on an extensive overseas exploration in what would become known as the Age of Exploration, which lasted till the middle of the seventeenth century. These voyages brought the explorers in contact with the local dwellers in the parts of the world they went to. The noticeable differences in the culture and morphology between themselves and the people they encountered, and between these different people in the different regions they travelled to culminated in scholarly endeavours aimed at understanding why this was so: were these people of the same breed of humans as ourselves or could they be from different human species? The resulting scholarship represents anthropology in its earliest stages. Some notable works during this period include those of German anthropologist Johann Friedrich Blumenbach *On the Natural Varieties of Mankind* (1775) and English biologist Charles Darwin *On the Origin of Species* (1859). Due to the basic nature of the research methods employed during this period, findings and conclusions were highly subjective.

The second period which began after World War II, in 1945, continuing to the present time, is marked by a slow but steady improvement in techniques resulting in a dramatic upsurge in both the quantity and quality of research.

Although studies conducted during both periods were respectively characterised by a relative degree of objectiveness, the overlapping period, from mid to late twentieth century, witnessed studies significantly influenced by a pervasive racial bias because it was during this time that the idea of race would become reinvented and subsequently politicised, most of which cast a negative shadow on Africa. During this era, opinions became divided among scholars, resulting in the aforementioned schools of thought: Out of Africa and Multiregional Continuity models. And the argument arose about "modern humans" descending from ancestors who had "evolved" in different regions after having migrated out of Africa where the first human species originated. This theory was based more on personal opinion rather than science and is yet to be substantiated scientifically. On the contrary, recent studies have debunked the key assumptions underlying the theory, notably those of Europeans and Asians descending from Neanderthals (*Homo neanderthalensis*) and Peking Man (*Homo erectus pekinensis*), respectively.

Neanderthals are named after one of the first sites where their fossils were discovered in the mid-nineteenth century, the Neander Valley, in today's Germany, while Peking Man is based on fossils discovered in 1923–1927 during excavations at a site near Beijing in China.

Thanks to advanced research techniques, the idea of any humans descending from Neanderthals can finally be rested because mitochondrial DNA (mtDNA) has now shown that humans and Neanderthals are distinct groups who are in no way related, further revealing the impossibility of an admixture through interbreeding. This was the finding in a study conducted by a team of researchers at the Max Planck Institute for Evolutionary Anthropology in Germany, which sequenced the mtDNA of the Neanderthal type specimen found in 1856 in the Neander Valley, determined from 92 clones derived from four independent extracts. The research team reported in 1999 that when the reconstructed sequence was analysed together with the previously determined DNA sequence, the Neanderthal mtDNA was found to fall outside a "phylogenetic tree" relating the mtDNAs of "contemporary humans." The report authors, which include S. Pääbo, director of the Department of Genetics at the institute, concluded that the results support the concept that the Neanderthal mtDNA "evolved separately from that of modern humans for a substantial amount of time and lends no support to the idea that they contributed mtDNA to contemporary modern humans." (Krings. M, H. Geisert, R.W. Schmitz, H. Krainitzki, and S. Pääbo. 1999. DNA sequence of the mitochondrial hyper variable region II from the Neanderthal type specimen.).

Furthermore, a different archaeological evidence, based on fossils from two caves in modern-day Israel (Amud and Kebara), and the Iberian Peninsula, has revealed Neanderthals and Homo sapiens overlapped in different parts of old Eurasia, for periods ranging from 10,000 to 55,000 years. Also, the lack of anatomical intermediates at such locations where Neanderthals and Homo sapiens are believed to have overlapped suggest that the two species, where they may have coexisted, did not interbreed, thus refuting any admixture assumptions. As with Neanderthals, so it is with Peking Man as another study also revealed the absence of any genetic link between them and human populations in Asia. A genetic survey produced in collaboration by a team led by researchers at Cambridge and Anglia Ruskin Universities found that there was no evidence of a genetic inheritance from Homo erectus by any living humans today. Finally, another research by a team of researchers from the University of Cambridge, England, led by Andrea Manica, an evolutionary ecologist, compared the skulls and DNA of human remains from around the world but did not find any evidence that humans living elsewhere in the world outside Africa contributed to the genetic make-up of modern human ancestors, concluding that modern humans have a single origin in Africa.

On the other hand, many research conducted using the most advanced techniques point to a single African origin of humans. The study of the origin of humans has progressed significantly from basic techniques during the eighteenth century to more sophisticated and highly advanced techniques in the twenty-first century. For instance, the predominance of skeletal anatomy gave way to a broader approach reflecting the integration of many disciplines. Molecular phylogenetic became central to the study of human origins by the end of the twentieth century, as well as methodological advances in geology and the life sciences. Radiometric dating techniques, the analysis of blood-serum protein as a proxy for genes, and the decoding of DNA have also come into application helping to address some of the fundamental issues in anthropology, particularly paleoanthropology. Advances in genetic research have contributed significantly in determining human origins, especially the sequencing of mitochondrial DNA. Mitochondrial DNA is the small circular chromosome found inside the mitochondria (organelles found in cells, which have often been regarded as the powerhouse of the cell) and is passed down from mothers to both male and female descendants. It is thus used to credibly determine basic maternal ancestry in both recent and ancient times. On the other hand, Y chromosome DNA is passed only from father to son and is used to ascertain patrilineal ancestry in modern and ancient times. A combination of the two types of DNA reveals a complete and accurate ancestral history. In his book, *Modern Humans: Their African Origin and Global Dispersal* (Columbia University Press. 2017), John F. Hoffecker, a fellow at the Institute of Arctic and Alpine Research, University of Colorado Boulder, Boulder, Colorado, USA, explained in great detail the basis for the Recent African Origin model. In a section of his book, Hoffecker states: "Our current understanding of modern human evolution is a product of the postwar transformation of paleoanthropology. It began with the discovery of fossils of anatomically modern humans in Africa that yielded radiometric data significantly older than those of fossils of modern humans outside Africa. The comparative age of the fossils became the basis of the Recent African Origin (RAO) model for Homo sapiens. In the late 1980s, the analysis of mitochondrial DNA (mtDNA) from a broad sample of living people indicated Africa as the source of maternal lineages outside Africa and provided an estimate for the time of divergence. This was followed by many other genetic studies and, eventually, analysis of some ancient DNA (aDNA) from dated skeletal remains in the Northern Hemisphere. New archaeological finds yielded evidence for the emergence of modern human cognitive faculties in Africa and offered clues to their role in the dispersal out of Africa." Hoffecker's aforementioned book is invaluable for anyone interested in studying more about human origins.

It is impossible including in this chapter every research done on the subject of human origins which attest to a single origin in Africa. However, the following is a small selection of some of the other investigations conducted using genetics, all of them confirming a single African origin for modern humans: (a) Studies of contemporary DNA, especially mtDNA, reveal that humans are astonishingly homogeneous with relatively little genetic variation (Ingram, M., H. Kaessmann, S. Pääbo, and U. Gyllensten. 2000. *Mitochondrial genome variation and the origin of modern humans* Nature Magazine, 408:708-713). (b) Work by Cann, Stoneking, and Wilson demonstrate that the highest level of genetic variation in mtDNA occurs in present African populations, implying that modern humans arose first in Africa and therefore had a longer time to accumulate genetic diversity.

By comparing the genetic distance between African populations and humans in other continents, they were also able to establish that modern populations of humans first appeared in Africa before any other part of the world (Cann, R.L, M. Stoneking, and A.C. Wilson. 1987. *Mitochondrial DNA and human evolution.* Nature Magazine, 325:32-36). (c) The Human Genome Project (HGP) has also determined that there is the same amount of genetic variation among individuals within a so-called racial group as there is between individuals in different racial groups. This means that there is no real genetic difference between Blacks and Whites or between Whites and Asians, or between any of the so-called races. (d) Scientists have confirmed that all human beings in the world today have a common ancestry in Africa through human genome mapping. By mapping the human genome, scientists have now also been able to establish the different waves and pattern of the outward migrations from Africa, which led to the other human settlements in other parts of the world. (e) A genetic survey produced by a collaborative team led by scholars at Cambridge and Anglia Ruskin Universities presents new DNA evidence confirming a single origin of modern humans in Africa, with results showing that Australia's aboriginal population sprang from the same tiny group of colonists along with their New Guinean neighbours. The research confirms the Out Of Africa hypothesis that all modern humans stem from a single group of Homo sapiens who emigrated from Africa many years ago. (f) The foregoing research also found that there was no evidence of a genetic inheritance from *Homo erectus*, indicating that the settlers did not mix and that these people (Australian aborigines and New Guineans), therefore, share the same direct ancestry as the other Eurasian peoples.

Suffice it to say that modern genetic evidence is overwhelmingly in favour of a single African origin.

Studies in other fields similarly confirm a single African origin. In anatomy, for instance, it is now established that the anatomical pattern of the modern population of humans existed first in Africa before any other part of the world. In 1967, a fossil-hunting team led by Paleoanthropologist Richard Leakey recovered human skull fragments and other remains from the Kibish Formation on the banks of Omo River in Ethiopia. The *Omo-Kibish I* skull, identified as robust-looking, was dated by archaeologist Karl W. Butzer to roughly 130,000 years ago—earlier than the modern population of humans were thought to be present anywhere. During the 1970s and 1980s, more modern human skeletal remains from East and South Africa—including Border Cave (South Africa), Florisbad (South Africa), Eliye Springs (Ethiopia), and Klasies River Mouth (South Africa)—were dated to time ranges which antedated the appearance of modern humans outside of Africa.

Based on these new evidences, at the International Congress of Human Palaeontology held in Nice, France in October 1982, British paleoanthropologists Michael Day and Christopher Stringer, and German anatomist Günter Bräuer argued for a recent African origin of modern humans, reasoning that modern humans appeared first in Africa and must therefore have spread from Africa to other parts of the world.

Studies in linguistics also point to a single African origin: The evolution of human languages has been traced to a source-language first spoken in Africa several years ago. A study led by Dr Quentin Atkinson of Auckland University analysed more than 500 languages and found they can be traced back to a long-forgotten dialect spoken by Stone Age human ancestors. Interestingly, the findings did not only pinpoint the origin of language to Africa but also reveal that speech evolved at least 100,000 years ago (much earlier than previously thought). The study, which has been welcomed by British evolutionary scientists, who also said it shed light on one of the most important moments in human evolution, provides further compelling evidence that modern humans existed in Africa, possibly 200,000 to 150,000 years ago, according to an article by David Derbyshire, published on Mail Online.

Although some scholars had argued that language evolved independently in different parts of the world, evidence now shows it evolved just once and that all languages descended from a single ancestral mother tongue. Dr Atkinson came up with fascinating evidence for a single African origin of language, which by extension also serves as evidence for a single African origin of modern population of humans. In a paper published in the journal Science on April 15, 2011, he counted the number of distinct sounds (phonemes) used in 504 languages from around the world and charted them on a map and found that the number of phonemes in a language tend to increase the closer it is to sub-Saharan Africa: For instance, English has 46 phonemes, Irish 69, Archi (Dagestan, Russia) 91, Mandarin (China) 32, Bengali 43, Igbo (Nigeria) 59, Xu (South Africa) 141, and the San bushmen (also in South Africa) has an overwhelming 200 distinct sounds. He also argues that these differences reflect the pattern of migration of modern humans from Africa several thousand years ago. The underlying reasoning here, according to Dr. Atkinson, is that languages change as they are handed down from generation to generation: In a large population, languages are likely to be relatively stable since there are more people to remember what and how previous generations spoke, while with smaller populations (such as a splinter group which sets off to find a new home elsewhere), there are more chances languages will change quickly and sounds lost from generation to generation. Professor Mark Pagel, an evolutionary biologist at Reading University, said the same effect could be observed in DNA: Modern-day Africans have been shown to have much greater genetic diversity than found in any other modern populations elsewhere in the world.

These are all parts of the overwhelming scientific evidence in support of a single African origin.

Establishing Africa as the place of origin for all humans in ancient and modern periods raises another important question about humans: What skin colour did the primary human ancestors have? This is particularly necessary because of the present concept of distinct human races, largely based on skin colour, mostly white and black.

The Primary Colour of Man

The answer to the question about the skin colour of the first humans should be obvious considering the place of their origin. Africa has always been home to people with dark skin, of the type now commonly referred to as "black", so it is only reasonable to assume that humans when they originated in Africa, were dark-skinned (or black). I had earlier presented the biblical account of creation in the Book of Genesis as my primary consideration relating to the origin of humans. However, since there is no direct reference in that account about the skin colour of the first male and female after both were created, I cannot make an authoritative claim based on that reference. Nonetheless, in Genesis 2:7, it is revealed that man was formed out of the "dust of the ground", and based on that alone, we can make an educated guess that man had to have been of brownish skin colour; the most common colour of the natural ground or soil.

Today, human skin colours are simply different shades of brown, with some dark enough to be regarded as black and some light enough to be seen as very light pink, but certainly not white. With this basic deduction made, we shall now explore scientific evidence relating to the skin colour of the first humans.

Again, modern research techniques have proven to be very helpful in this regard. An international collaboration involving researchers from different universities—Tartu (in Estonia), Oxford (in England), and Stanford, California (in the USA)—who contributed key data and expertise, analysed the mtDNA and Y chromosome DNA of Aboriginal Australians and Melanesians from New Guinea which was then compared with various DNA patterns associated with early humans. The results revealed that both groups share the same genetic features already linked to the exodus of modern humans from Africa a very long time ago. Geneticist Dr. Peter Forster, who led the research, states as follows: "Although it has been speculated that the populations of Australia and New Guinea came from the same ancestors, the fossil record differs so significantly it has been difficult to prove. For the first time, this evidence gives us a genetic link showing that the Australian Aboriginal and New Guinean populations are descended directly from the same specific group of people who emerged from the African migration." This means that if we want to determine the skin colour of those humans who first originated in Africa before subsequently migrating outwards, we only have to look at the indigenous peoples of Australia and New Guinea. Well, these people are black!

The doubt which existed relating to a common ancestry for Aboriginal Australians and their counterparts in New Guinea has also been rested due to a definitive conclusion from another genetic survey produced by a collaborative team led by scholars at the Cambridge and Anglia Ruskin Universities. Based on new DNA evidence, the survey determined that Australia's aboriginal population sprang from the same tiny group of colonists along with their New Guinean neighbours.

The doubt which existed about a common ancestry for the indigenous populations of New Guinea and Australia was based on "apparent inconsistencies in the evidence available in Australia," which is also cited by some scientists who argue for a multiregional ancestry. This inconsistency is represented by the striking difference in the skeletal and tool remains found in Australia when compared with those found elsewhere along the "coastal expressway"—the route through South Asia believed to be the one used by the early settlers who migrated through that region. Based on this, some proponents of the multiregional continuity theory had argued that the difference either existed because the early colonists interbred with the local Homo erectus population, or there was possibly a subsequent secondary migration from Africa.

The collaborative study by the researchers from Cambridge and Anglia Ruskin universities, reported in an online article published on May 8, 2007, on phys.org, found no evidence of any genetic inheritance from Homo erectus, and also that both groups of settlers in the region (Melanesians and Australian aborigines) did not mix, and therefore share the same direct ancestry as the other Eurasian peoples. Furthermore, whereas the reason behind the observed differences in skeletal and tool remains had remained previously unknown, the aforementioned collaborative study also provided some insight: The DNA patterns of the Australian and Melanesian populations show both to have evolved in relative isolation. The two groups also share certain genetic characteristics not found beyond Melanesia, thus suggesting that there was very little gene flow into Australia after the original migration. Dr. Toomas Kivisild, from Cambridge University Department of Biological Anthropology, who co-authored a research report published in an issue of Proceedings of the National Academy of Sciences, states: "The evidence points to relative isolation after the initial arrival, which would mean any significant developments in skel-etal form and tool use were not influenced by outside source. There was probably a minor secondary gene flow into Australia while the land bridge from New Guinea was still open, but once it was submerged the population was apparently isolated for thousands of years. The differences in the archaeological record are probably the result of this, rather than any secondary migration or breeding."

Eliminating the possibility of a secondary migratory wave direct from Africa into Australasia, as well as establishing a direct common ancestry for the indigenous peoples in the region, ensures we are left in no doubt about the skin colour of the first humans to inhabit Africa, from whom the rest of humanity descended—black (based on contemporary classification).

The next logical question, I suppose, would be: How did the "white" skin come about? Needless pointing out that the term "white" in relation to human skin colour is a misnomer because no human skin colour can be matched with the colour white on a colour chat. There is, however, a natural explanation for how people who were previously dark-skinned could have descendants with much lighter tones.

The answer is melanin. Melanin is the substance that, when present in the body, causes the skin to be dark. It is produced in the body aided by high ultraviolet (UV) ray in tropical climates such as Africa. In temperate climates, such as in Europe and parts of Asia, the low level of UV rays makes it very hard producing melanin in the body. Prolonged exposure in such regions would naturally limit the amount of melanin the body can produce, meaning that the skin becomes lighter with time. When this happens over several generations, descendants of originally dark skinned people would naturally become light-skinned, aided by the natural process of gene mutation through which humans adapt to new and harsh natural conditions.

My theory is that the lighter skin tone evolved as humans migrated from Africa, travelling further away from tropical climate regions into temperate regions. I believe that the process would have been initiated in the parts of Asia where the climate is predominantly temperate, such as the northern region.

There is evidence that the first settlers of the northern parts of Europe, who had crossed over from Northern Asia, had lighter skin. A study published in the journal Science by Ann Gibbons, on April 2, 2015, based on a paper presented the week before it was published at the 84th Annual Meeting of the American Association of Physical Anthropologists, has offered dramatic evidence of recent evolution in skin colour in Europe, and showed that most modern Europeans do not look much like those of 8,000 years ago. An international team of researchers sequenced the genomes of ancient populations and, by comparing key parts of the DNA across the genomes of 83 ancient individuals from archaeological sites throughout Europe, reported earlier in 2015 that today's Europeans are a mix of the blending of at least three ancient populations of hunter-gatherers and farmers who moved into Europe in separate migrations over the past 8,000 years. With respect to skin colour, the team found a patchwork of evolution in different places, and three separate genes that produce the lighter shade of skin tone, telling a complex story for how European's skin evolved to be much lighter during the past 8,000 years. The study revealed that the hunter-gatherers who first settled in Northern Europe possessed the gene variants responsible for the light skin. Seven people from the 7,700-year-old Motala archaeological site in southern Sweden had light skin gene variants SLC24A5 and SLC45A2. They also had a third gene, HERC2/OCA2, which causes blue eyes and may also contribute to light skin and blond hair. What this study also revealed is that the European continent had not always been predominantly light-skinned. Although the first settlers in Northern Europe had light skin, those who first settled in the south had dark skin and were the first to settle in Europe, having arrived there around 40,000 years ago. Ann states in her article: "The modern humans who came out of Africa to originally settle Europe about 40,000 years ago are presumed to have dark skin, which is advantageous in sunny latitudes." New data from the study confirm that as recent as about 8500 years ago, the early hunter-gatherers in Spain, Luxembourg, and Hungary had darker skin and lacked versions of two genes—SLC24A5 and SLC45A2—which cause depigmentation. The situation in Europe about 8,500 years ago was that of a mixture of ancient hunter-gatherers in the far north with very light skin and blue-eyes and those in central and southern Europe who had dark skin. This remained the case till about 8,000 years ago before the first farmers arrived on the continent from nearby Asia, who also carried both genes for light skin. As these new arrivals interbred with the indigenous hunter-gatherers, one of their light-skin genes swept through Europe, leading to the lighter skin emerging in central and southern European. The other gene variant SLC45A2, was at low levels until about 5,800 years ago, when it swept up to high frequency.

This study also confirms the skin tone of the humans who first lived in Africa to be black and offers a scientific explanation for the lightening of the human skin.

The foregoing all further demonstrate that the concept of race based on skin colour is highly flawed because the people who are now referred to as white descended from ancestors who were at some point black. This means that there could not be any real genetic difference between those who are now white and those now black, at least not more than there are within each group. This is what recent research studies have revealed as modern scholarship continue to debunk almost all spurious scientific theories put forward in past centuries, particularly those based heavily on pervasive and biased ideas rather than credible and verifiable evidence. The concept of distinct races within humanity is perhaps one of the most flawed of such theories and has been seriously challenged and discredited by modern scholars. For instance, Anthropologist Charles Loring Brace IV, who noted that skin tone is not limited by geography, in his book *Evolution in an Anthropological View* (AltaMira Press. 2000), writes: "To this day, skin color grades by imperceptible means from Europe southward around the eastern end of the Mediterranean and up to the Nile into Africa. From one end of this range to the other, there is no hint of a skin color boundary, and yet the spectrum runs from the lightest in the world at the northern edge to as dark as it is possible for humans to be at the equator." Colour, therefore, is not a valid basis for any classification of humans into distinct groups, particularly of a racial nature.

Race is now widely accepted among scholars as an ideology. The term "Ideology of Race" was first used by Anthropologist Audrey Smedley in her book *Race in North America: Origin and Evolution of a Worldview* (Westview Press. 2011), in which she postulated different races to be primordial, natural, enduring, and distinct. Although she was very wrong. Nonetheless, based on this ideology, innate predispositions have been attributed to different population groups in a completely unscientific manner, resulting in prejudice and stereotyping. The tide is gradually shifting as more scholars now refute race, highlighting it as a social construct, all due to new evidence. In 1972, genetic findings began to be incorporated into the scientific investigation of race and in the same year geneticist Richard Lewontin published an important study of variation in protein types in human blood based on a study population group which he had divided into seven races—West Eurasian, African, East Asian, South Asian, Native American, Oceanian, and Australian. Lewontin found that about 85 percent of variation in the protein types could be accounted for by variation within populations and races, and only 15 percent by variation across them. Lewontin thus concluded that to the extent that there was variation among humans, most of it was because of "differences between individuals" rather than between population groups. He stated that human populations "are remarkably similar to each other" from a genetic point of view. His findings are corroborated by the Human Genome Project (HGP), which was concluded in 2003. It was determined by the Project that there is the same amount of genetic variation among individuals within a so-called racial group as there is between individuals in different racial groups, meaning there is no real genetic difference between Blacks and Whites or between Whites and Asians or between any of these groups. Also, Kenneth K. Kidd, a professor of Genetics and Psychiatry at Yale Medical School, says that work by others and himself over the last decade has driven a spike into the heart of the idea of genetic racial differences, stating: "In lectures, I now say that human races do not exist if by race you mean a discrete category, a qualitatively different subgroup of humanity. When I look at DNA, I see no racial differences. There tend to be more DNA variations within each population group than between groups, and such variation is present broadly around the world within every population. This contradicts conventional wisdom of earlier this century when there was a tendency to think of populations as monomorphic with rare variants." Furthermore, in June 2000, when a report based on the HGP was presented during an elaborate ceremony at the White House in the USA, scientists involved in the project opined that race was more a social construct than a valid scientific concept. The team of scientists had set out to assemble the first complete human genome, which was a composite of several individuals, deliberately sourcing samples from people who identified themselves as members of different races. Craig Venter, a pioneer of DNA sequencing, and Francis Collins of the US National Institute of Health jointly announced the mapping of the human genome at the 2000 White House ceremony. Venter found that although the genetic variation within human species is on the order of one to three percent, instead of the previously assumed one percent, the types of variations do not support the notion of genetically defined races. Venter concludes as follows: "Race is a social concept. It is not a scientific one. There are no bright lines (that would stand out) if we could compare all the sequenced genomes of everyone on the planet." In September 2012, another group of scientists announced the results of five years of work in unravelling the secrets of how the genome operates. The ENCODE project, as the study is known, found that at least eighty percent of the genome is important, thereby dispensing with any idea that human DNA is repeating sequences with no functionality. DNA has proved very helpful and influential in helping science provide crucial answers to age-long questions about race. Through studies in DNA, including mtDNA and ancient DNA (aDNA), it has been possible to conclude that race has no valid biological basis.

In an article published in the journal Science on February 4, 2016, four scholars say racial categories are weak proxies for genetic diversity and need to be phased out. Michael Yudell, a Professor of Public Health at Drexel University in Philadelphia, USA, who took part in the study, says: "It's a concept we think is too crude to provide useful information, it's a concept that has social meaning that interferes in the scientific understanding of human genetic diversity and it's a concept that we are not the first to call upon moving away from." Commenting on the findings and recommendations of the report, Svante Pääbo, a biologist and

Director of the Max Planck Institute for Evolutionary Anthropology in Germany, states: "Essentially, I could not agree more with the authors. What the study of complete genomes from different parts of the world has shown is that even between Africa and Europe, for example, there is not a single absolute genetic difference, meaning no single variant where all Africans have one variant and all Europeans another one, even when recent migration is disregarded. It is all a question of differences in how frequent different variants are on different continents and in different regions." In one example which shows genetic differences were not fixed along racial lines, the full genomes of two scientists from the USA, James Watson and Craig Venter, both of European ancestry, were compared to that of a Korean scientist, Seong-Jin Kim: The result showed that Watson and

Venter shared fewer variants in their genetic sequences than they each shared with Kim.

The concept of distinct human races has authoritatively been debunked. It is not fit for any useful purpose except as a tool for control and marginalisation. Therefore, its application should be discontinued in any form and in every way.

Humanity has a single origin in Africa, and with the skin colour now popularly referred to as blacks. This much is proven, scientifically and otherwise.

CHAPTER TWO

Migration

Humans are itinerant by nature, having been created to be fruitful, multiply, and replenish (or fill) the earth (Genesis 1: 28), which means that having originated in Africa, our primary ancestors were not expected to remain confined in that region in perpetuity. Instead, they were meant to explore the whole world. And they did! The presence of human settlements in every continent of the world is ample evidence they did. How long they lived in Africa before deciding to try other shores is not known. However, it is reasonable to assume that they would have first expanded across the African landmass—including the part of today's Middle East, which is on the same tectonic plate as today's Africa—before attempting to crossover to other landmasses.

Based on the Book of Genesis, the first major wave of migration occurred after the event described in the eleventh chapter when humans attempted to construct a tower in the city of Babel. To prevent them from achieving their purpose, which was founded on disobedience, God confused their language and caused them to be scattered as recorded in the eighth verse: *So the LORD scattered them abroad from thence upon the face of all the earth: and they left off to build the city* (KJV).

Babel was a city in the ancient Babylonian Empire, which existed as a dominant power in the Mesopotamian area during antiquity. The empire is believed to have encompassed a vast region that included today's Iraq and Syria, implying that humans had already expanded across Africa to her far north eastern parts before the mass exodus out of Africa. However, this biblical account is limited in information regarding the actual migration—the routes taken and the destinations settled as a result. Fortunately, through scientific research, some theories have been put forward, some of which are plausible.

The Human Genome Project (HGP), launched by the US government in 1990 and completed in 2003 as an international scientific research project, remains the world's largest collaborative biological project. Its objectives included the identification and mapping of all genes of the human genome from both a physical and functional standpoint. Data from the HGP has aided research in various fields, including anthropology. By mapping the genome of the present population, establishing the pattern of the first major migratory waves out of Africa has been possible. The Genographic Project of the National Geographic Society is one of the first to use genetics in tracing the human migratory pattern and has come up with a possible sequence and route for the initial migration out of Africa. Molecular anthropology uses modern DNA to understand certain aspects of the history of human species, including origins and migratory patterns and routes. Certain pieces of human DNA remain unchanged from generation to generation. Often, a mutation can occur in these DNA segments, which are passed down unmixed to subsequent generations. Science Manager at the Genographic Project, Molecular Anthropologist Miguel Vilar, explained how it works: "We can use the mutations in these genetic markers to calculate how populations are related and estimate when populations might have diverged. The more mutations two populations share, the more closely related they are. Through this process we can retrace our past as far as 150,000 years, or roughly 5,000 generations." By mapping the appearance and frequency of genetic markers in modern populations, the project was able to create a picture of when and where ancient humans moved around the world, thereby demonstrating how these great migrations eventually "led the descendants of a small group of Africans to occupy even the farthest reaches of the Earth."

The Journey across the World

Evidence suggests the exodus out of Africa occurred in successive migratory waves—it is believed there were two major waves, with multiple minor waves occurring within each. Based on available research, the following is a rough timeline of human settlements outside Africa: The old Australasian landmass had been settled about 70,000 years ago by migrants using a north-easterly route from Africa, at a time when Australia and Papua New Guinea were still joined to the same landmass. It is unclear whether this journey was made directly from the African landmass or the migrants first crossed into the Eurasian landmass before journeying further. However, new evidence was discovered in Kimberley, Australia in 2004 by an expert in Australian rock art, Grahame Walsh, of paintings of ocean-faring boats—the oldest painting of a boat anywhere in the world—meaning that a direct ocean voyage directly from Africa could have been possible even then. It is now believed this journey was planned, not accidental, because evidence suggests the entourage included men and women sizeable enough to found a new population at their destination and was made using ocean-faring boats constructed for the purpose. They arrived via northern Australasia when Australia and Papua New Guinea were still joined together before venturing deeper inland, guided by rivers, where they found gi-ant mammals, birds, and reptiles ripe for hunting; fortunately, no other humans to challenge them. Alas, this intrepid group of explorers had stumbled upon a new continent, and they had it all to themselves! These are the people the indigenous populations in present Australia, and Melanesia are descended from, as proven by research. However, such a journey being made directly from Africa was previously inconceivable due to the vast distance and oceans between the two continental landmasses. That was until the discovery by Walsh in 2004 revealed that the existing technology during the period was not as primitive and basic as imagined but was rather advanced enough for the construction of ocean vessels. He found two paintings of ocean-going boats, one with 23 people on board, the other 29. The crucial detail in the paintings discovered is the high prow of the boat, which would have been unnecessary in boats used in calm inland waters, thereby suggesting that this was a boat used in the stormier and rough open ocean. Prior to this discovery, it was initially assumed that the first settlers of Australasia did so by travelling through the "Coastal Expressway" in Eurasia using boats. Recent evidence has proven this assumption wrong, including the finding in 2011 that the aboriginal peoples of Australia are more closely related to present populations in Africa than they are to present Eurasian populations genetically. Another study discovered through DNA analysis that the aboriginal populations in Australia and Papua New Guinea evolved in relative isolation, and both share certain genetic characteristics not found beyond Melanesia.

The old Eurasia, on her part, became settled during different multiple waves which occurred within the First Wave, with settlements expanding as far as the most south-easterly region of today's Asia by around 63,000 years ago, based on remains excavated in Laos. A discovery was made in 2012 of human skull fragments in a limestone cave in northern Laos, which dated back to 46,000 and 63,000 years ago, indicating that settlements in old Eurasia had expanded to the most south-easterly part of today's Asia by that period. Another major wave, the Second Wave, subsequently occurred within Eurasia several years after the first via an inland route resulting in more settlements across today's Asia. From these base camps in the Asian part of old Eurasia, further expansion occurred into the northern latitudes of Asia and subsequently into Northern Europe.

It is instructive to note that it would have been during this stage in our migratory history that the lighter skin now referred to as "white" began to be developed. Around 40,000 years ago, human settlements had expanded across old Eurasia up to the southern part of today's Europe, having travelled directly from

Africa. As previously highlighted in the preceding chapter, these first settlers of today's Europe were dark-skinned because they lacked versions of two genes—SLC24A5 and SLC45A2—which causes depigmentation, and also, the dark skin remained dominant in the region till about 8,500 years ago, based on a study done on samples found in Spain, Luxembourg, and Hungary. Around 8,500 years ago, the northern region of Europe had also been settled by migrants travelling from the northern region of today's Asia, who by the time of their arrival already possessed the lighter skin, having already been in possession of the light skin gene variants SLC24A5 and SLC45A2, and also a third gene HERC2/OCA2 which causes blue eyes and may also contribute to light skin and blond hair. Europe, as at 8,000 years ago, was predominantly light-skinned up north and dark-skinned down south till a fresh batch of migrants, farmers from nearby Asia, arrived in the south about 5,800 years ago, who also possessed the light skin gene variant SLC45A2, which assisted in the widespread of the light skin across Europe through interbreeding.

This is corroborated by evidence found in the 10,000-year-old Cheddar Man, Britain's oldest complete skeleton discovered in 1903 in Gough's Cave in Somerset's Cheddar Gorge in England, who was discovered to have dark brown skin and blue eyes. The new study, reported early in 2018, was conducted by researchers from London's Natural History Museum who extracted DNA from Cheddar Man, while a University College London team of researchers analysed the genome, including gene variants associated with hair, eye and skin colour. When a facial reconstruction was done based on the results obtained from the genetic analysis, using cutting-edge technologies, the team discovered that the Stone Age Briton not only had blue eyes and dark-brown or black skin but also dark hair, with a small probability that it was curlier than average. Science editor at the BBC News website, Paul Rincon, who authored an article on the study reports: "This combination might appear striking to us today, but it was common appearance in western Europe during this period." In the article, Rincon quoted Professor Chris Stringer, the museum's research leader in human origins, thus: "I've been studying the skeleton of Cheddar Man for about 40 years. So to come face-to-face with what this guy could have looked like—and that striking combination of the hair, the face, the eye colour and that dark skin: something a few years ago we couldn't have imagined and yet that's what the scientific data show." Worthy of note is that Cheddar Man's genome reveals he was closely related to the ancient hunter-gatherers whose remains were found in Spain, Luxembourg and Hungary. Interestingly, Cheddar Man has also been generically linked with some modern residents of the village Cheddar in Somerset, England, where his remains were excavated. A previous study on Cheddar Man done late in 1990 by Oxford University geneticist Brian Sykes also analysed DNA from Cheddar Man. Prof. Sykes sequenced mitochondrial DNA from one of Cheddar Man's molars and compared the ancient genetic information with DNA from twenty living residents of Cheddar village and found two matches. BBC's Paul Rincon writes that the result is consistent with the approximately ten percent of Europeans who share the same mitochondrial DNA type. Cheddar Man, therefore, further proves that a person with "white skin" or a white person could be descended from a dark-skinned or black ancestor. Cheddar Man is also proof that Britain was formerly settled by dark-skinned migrants before the arrival of light-skinned migrants in the area.

Around 50,000 years ago, the old American landmass had been settled through the southern region by migrants travelling directly from Australasia. This is based on new evidence. It had previously been believed that the first settlers in the old Americas were those migrants who settled in the northern region having travelled from Siberia (in Eurasia), but that the actual crossing through Beringia occurred around 24,000 years ago, long after settlers had arrived in the south. The Beringia crossing occurred following the Last Glacial Maximum (LGM), the most recent time during the Last Glacial Period when ice sheets were at their greatest extent resulting in a hypothetical land bridge—Bering Strait—which linked Eurasia with the North American continent of today. This bridge was formed around 24,000 years ago and existed till about 10,000 years ago. These migrants who first arrived the northern region eventually expanded, reaching the tip of the southern region about 15,000 years ago.

However, it is now known that the Beringia crossing is not responsible for the first settlement in the old Americas: A 2007 genetic study discovered some components of the mtDNA of Native Americans not present in Asia, which greatly challenged the Beringia hypothesis. The study analysed genetic variations in the DNA of present Native Americans, which was compared with the variations in Asia, and found the same rare pattern appeared in all the Native Americans studied but rarely appeared in Asians. Consequently, a modified hypothesis was proposed—the Beringian Standstill Hypothesis—based on the thesis that a genetically isolated population persisted in Beringia during the Last Glacial Maximum (LGM) before subsequently dispersing to North and South America during the post-LGM period. Proponents of this new theory argue that this "standstill" helped the isolated population group become genetically distinct from those they had left behind in Siberia thousands of years earlier. In other words, during the standstill at Beringia, "they differentiated from Asians and started becoming Native Americans," according to Geneticist and Biological Anthropologist Connie Mulligan of the University of Florida, Gainesville, USA, who took part in the 2007 study. Although debates had been ongoing over a very long time relating to the possibility that settlers arrived in the old Americas from different areas and times, Mulligan nonetheless insisted on a single crossing via Beringia, using the new standstill hypothesis as a justification. A standstill at Beringia is yet to be confirmed through research and so remains an assumption.

In 2015, however, another study presented evidence supporting that the old Americas was first settled through the south and earlier than the northern crossing through Beringia, thus confirming more than one founding population in the region. The team of researchers who carried out this study found that some indigenous populations of the Americas have distinct genetic links in common with people of Australia, Papua New Guinea and the Andaman Islands. They found a small degree of Australasian genetic ancestry among some Native American populations in South and Central America, based on genomic data. Another study reported in 2014, further challenges the idea the old Americas was first settled through the northern region.

Excavations in the Serra da Capivara site in Brazil yielded some stone tools that proved humans existed in the region as early as 22,000 years ago, upending the earlier assumption that humans first arrived the Southern Region of the old Americas between 15,000 and 13,000 years ago travelling from the North. In the rock shelters where prehistoric humans once lived, hidden paintings were discovered, some of which are thought to be more than 9,000 years old and perhaps even more ancient. Dr. Guidon, who visited the site in the company of fellow archaeologists in the 1970s, recalls: "These were stunning compositions, people and animals together, not just figures alone." Some of the paintings found at the site depicted images of giant armadillos, which had died out before the last Ice Age, implying those who made the paintings had existed before the last Ice Age.

Aside from the paintings, what the excavators found when they started digging in the shadows of the rock art contribute a pivotal re-evaluation of human history in the hemisphere. Researchers unearthed stone tools and charcoal, proving that humans reached current Northeast Brazil as early as between 50,000 and 22,000 years ago. Lucia (or Luzia), an eleven thousand-year-old human skull, the oldest skull ever found in the old Americas, was found in the region of Lagoa Santa, in the vicinity of Belo Horizonte in what is now Brazil. An evolutionary anthropologist at the University of São Paulo, Walter Neves, who later analysed the skull, concluded that Native Americans (or ancient Americans) resembled aboriginal Australians more than they did Asians. Furthermore, palaeontologists in Uruguay published findings in November 2013, indicating that humans hunted giant sloths in the area about 30,000 years ago. Also, in Brazil's caatinga, a semi-arid region of mesas and canyons, archaeologists building on decades of earlier excavations in 2013 declared that they had found artefacts at a rock shelter showing humans had arrived in what is now South America almost 10,000 years before Clovis hunters began appearing in what is now North America. Another study published in Nature in 2013 found that the indigenous people who lived in southeastern Brazil in the late 1800s shared some genetic sequences with Polynesians, based on an analysis of their remains.

An observation that had continually puzzled scholars was the predominance of the Clovis genetic trait in present Native American populations. The Clovis people have Asian ancestry, and the predominance of their genetic trait in Native Americans was seen as proof the latter also had Asian ancestry. The challenge was if the first settlers in the old Americas descended from indigenous populations in Australasia, how then was it that they left little genetic traits within present Native American people? Hence, some scholars still maintain that the Beringia crossing was responsible for the only founding population of the old Americas.

The mystery behind the predominance of the Clovis genetic trait has finally been unravelled: Analysis of remains from the site in Brazil where Luzia was found shows that the initial settlers in the south of the old Americas, who had originally travelled from Australasia, were most likely annihilated by the later settlers who came from the north after they eventually arrived at the south where both groups met. Skulls dug from the site from a depth equivalent to 9,000 to 12,000 years ago, when extensively analysed, showed they possessed features that closely resembled those of the aboriginal populations of Australia and Melanesia. Walter Neves, who analysed dozens of skulls from the site, including that of Luzia, comments: "The measurement shows that Lucia was anything but mongoloid." Forensic artist Richard Neave of the University of Manchester, England, who created a face for Luzia based on a CAT scan reports: "It has all the features of a negroid face." The deduction here is that up to about 9,000 years ago, descendants of the initial settlers from Australasia were still present in the south of old Americas. However, between 9,000 to 7,000 years ago, the skulls upon analysis revealed exclusively mongoloid features as opposed to the exclusively negroid features observed from skulls dating between 12,000 and 9,000 years ago. Combining this evidence with evidence from rock art discovered at the site of increasing violence during this period, a gory picture of annihilation emerges. The only evidence of any survivors came from Terra del Fuego, the islands at the remotest southern tip of South America. According to an article on BBC News online, the ancient Fuegians who lived stone-age-style lives until this century, show hybrid skull features that could have resulted from interbreeding between the Australian and Asian migrant groups.

Thus the first globetrotting was completed, with human settlements established in every continent. Humans did not stop migrating once every continental landmass was settled; instead, migration has become an integral part of humanity. Subsequent migratory waves have occurred over time resulting in significant changes in the demography of continental populations up to the present period.

While it is impossible to document every wave of migration and their impact on the different continents because available records are limited, we shall explore some recorded major waves that significantly impacted the demography of the different continents.

Other Journeys across the World

Migration of humans is continuous, both in past and present periods, as people have continually moved from place to place driven by one or more reasons, usually survival and the need for better conditions. Our foremost ancestors migrated from their place of origin, in Africa, settling and populating the rest of the world's landmasses now referred to as continents.

It is instructive to note that our continents acquired their respective names in a relatively more recent historical period; it is unknown whether or not the first humans had a name for today's Africa or the other landmasses they would eventually settle since records don't exist for that period in human history. Also, some names have changed over time. For instance, the then Eurasia is now broken into Europe and Asia, Australasia is now Australia/Oceania, Americas is now North America and South America. Although Africa retains its name, part of its North East is now reclassified as the Middle East. It is also important to note that continental classification is not entirely scientific but can be arbitrary in some cases. For instance, the Middle East, which is not on a separate tectonic plate, Europe, which comprises of the UK, Republic of Ireland and other islands not directly connected to the main tectonic plate, North America and South America are now classified as different continents although both are part of the same tectonic plate, while Australia/Oceania present a unique situation where multiple islands and separate landmasses have been grouped into a continent.

It is important to understand that the present continental classification is vague, at the least, and not based on science. Hence, the term region is now being used instead of continents by some Geography scholars. However, continent would be used here based on a contemporary concept.

How the continents became settled for the first time, when and by whom, was previously outlined, and we shall now revisit each region to see how the demography has changed over time. Note, however, that this exercise is not comprehensive or chronological. Instead, it is highly summarised and primarily for the sole purpose of revealing how migration has shaped our world and continues to do so.

We noted earlier that Australasia was first settled by the ancestors of the present indigenous populations in that region, including those who came directly from Africa and the latter migrants who arrived through Asia, meaning that the present-day continent of Australia/Oceania was predominantly aboriginal initially. The demography of the region today is significantly different with the original aboriginal populations now a minority. The shift resulted from a gradual process that began around the sixteenth century as explorers from Europe began to travel the world. Portuguese explorers were the first to arrive in the region, and they began to settle in the Maluku Islands (or the Moluccas). They were followed by Spanish explorers who landed on the Mariana Islands (or the Marianas) before expanding into nearby islands, such as The Caroline

Islands and Papua New Guinea, with time. By the seventeenth century, Dutch explorers landed in New Zealand and Australia but did not initially establish any permanent settlements. They were followed by British explorers who had become a dominant force in this subsection of Australia/Oceania by late eighteenth century. In 1788, the British being the dominant colonial power in the area, established settler colonies in Australia and New Zealand. The first British colony was founded in New South Wales, which at the time included New Zealand. New Zealand became a separate colony in 1840. This "scramble" in Australia/Oceania was driven mainly by political rivalry between competing European empires as they embarked on expansion under imperialism. Related to this was the search for trade opportunities, including routes, which assisted in creating wealth—a vital tool for empire-building.

The presence of these modern Europeans helped to significantly alter the regional demography, including the introduction of a new mixed population group resulting from interbreeding. Today, people of modern European descent remain a primary ethnic group in much of Australia/Oceania, constituting a majority in some areas, notably Australia and New Zealand, where they are also dominant politically and economically. Inward and outward migration continued in the region over time, which resulted in introducing other ethnicities in the existing mix. From the late-1970s, there was a significant increase in migrants from Africa and Asia into the region resulting in the present diverse and multicultural mix.

Asia, once part of Eurasia, was first settled through its southern region by migrants who crossed over from Northeastern Africa before subsequently expanding across the continent up to its northernmost region. Asia during this initial stage was solely aboriginal and predominantly dark-skinned before the emergence of the lighter skin tone, which is believed to have occurred in the temperate northern region of the continent. Over time, with inward and outward migration, the demography began to change, gradually and then significantly.

Modern research has revealed indigenous Asian populations—including India, Japan, and China—are strikingly different morphologically to modern Asian populations, particularly in facial structure, skull dimension, and skin tone. Physical features such as an upward orientation of the cheekbone, a broad face with limited projection, shovel-shaped incisors, and flattened nasal bones and a broad nose, common in modern Asians, have been shown to be relatively recent in the continent. Analysis of skulls and other remains discovered at archaeological sites in Baoji, China, and in the Huaxia region (of ancient China) revealed some of these physical features began to appear in the region as recently as about 7,000 years ago. Going further back in time revealed a different story. A study reported in association with the Australian Museum found fossil specimens in different parts of the region with features not common in present populations: The specimens include the skull of a middle-aged man found in a cave in Liujiang district of Guangxi, China, dating 25,000–10,000 years ago, another skull found in the Upper Cave 101 of Zhoukoudian, China (discovered with two more skulls and bones from about eight individuals), also dating 25,000–10,000 years ago, and Minatogowa 1 skull, a male skeleton found in 1970 in Japan, dating 17,000 years ago. These human remains all displayed physical features commonly associated with Africa, leading scholars to link them with migration out of Africa.

Chinese historiography also reveals that some local people were referred to as "black dwarfs" by ancient Chinese historians, people who were known to be diminutive, broad-nosed, and dark-skinned with curly hair. The black dwarfs were still present in China during the Qing Dynasty, which existed between 1644 to 1911.

Genetic studies suggest a significant population reduction in indigenous populations about 10,000 years ago, which has been linked to the spread of agriculture in the region. It is instructive to note that after the initial expansion in Asia, which had occurred from the south to the north, other migration subsequently occurred southwards from the north, after the "mongoloid" features had emerged in the north, leading to an admixture of genes through interbreeding resulting in a new group mixed with both "negroid" and "mongoloid" features. In southern Asia, the Dravidian people, a dark-skinned indigenous population, constituted a majority before the second millennium BC. But from around 1500 BC, several migratory waves which brought the Indo-Aryan peoples from Northern and Central Asia into the southern region resulted in a drastic reduction of the Dravidian majority. With time, the Indo-Aryan group became the majority.

During the fifteenth century, European explorers began to arrive in the Indian subcontinent, starting with Portuguese explorers. Vasco da Gama, a Portuguese explorer, became the first European to re-establish direct trade links with India since ancient Roman times, following his arrival towards the end of the fifteenth century. Trading rivalries in imperial Europe resulted in people from other European countries migrating to the region, notably the Dutch, British and French. And the scramble for Old India was on. The British and French Empires competed for regional dominance during the eighteenth century, after the Mughal empire became disintegrated and the Maratha empire severely weakened. The British emerged victors and by the mid-nineteenth century had gained overall control of the subcontinent, which encouraged more migration into the region by the British, as well as interbreeding.

In East Asia, the first documented government in ancient China was the Shang (or Chiang) dynasty, which existed during the second millennium BC. Although the first to be recorded, Shang is traditionally known as the second ancient Chinese dynasty and successor to the unrecorded first dynasty known as Xia. The Xia's existence remains a mystery, as there is no consensus among historians that it truly existed. Some historians propose that Xia was invented, as a pretext, by the Zhou, who conquered and succeeded the Shang in an attempt to justify their conquest of the latter—by noting that as the Shang conquered the Xia, so did the Zhou conquer the Shang. Tradition also has it that the Shang were overthrown because they were a people different from the Zhou, who are widely acknowledged as the first Chinese dynasty with "mongoloid" features. The first two dynasties are believed to be founded by people who had "negroid" features. The Shang were also referred to by another name, "Nakhi"—literally, "Blackman." The Qin dynasty succeeded the Zhou during the late third century BC and were succeeded by the Han dynasty in 206 BC. Hans migration into mainland China from coastal areas significantly increased during the dynasty, with successive migration occurring later, including in the 700s when there was an influx of Hans migrants from northern to southern China. The Hans now constitute a significant ethnic majority in today's China, accounting for about 92 percent of the total population of mainland China and about 95 percent of the population of Taiwan.

The old Americas, or today's North and South America, was first settled through the southern region and subsequently through the northern region, resulting in two founding populations of diverse ethnicity, with both groups converging in the south after the migrants from the north eventually arrived at the south, resulting in some of the original southern population migrating northwards having been displaced by the new arrivals. The historiography of the Americas reveals that by the seventh century, the Taino people, an indigenous population in the region, already existed in some islands neighbouring North America including Cuba, Trinidad, Jamaica, Haiti, Dominican Republic, and Puerto Rico, and are believed to have migrated to the region from South America. Before the fifteenth century, the population of the Americas was predominantly indigenous, but this began to change after the fifteenth century when explorers from Europe started arriving in the area.

Italian explorer Christopher Columbus, navigating under a Spanish sponsorship, accidentally landed on the island of Hispaniola in North America while attempting to find a new trade route to East Asia. He thought he had landed in Asia but was wrong; he was in the Americas! This "accident" subsequently culminated in conquest, large-scale exploration, and colonisation of the Americas by European powers. Spain being Columbus' sponsor, was the first to settle and colonise the largest areas, from North America and neighbouring islands (including the

Caribbean) to the southern tip of South America. France also founded colonies in eastern North America, a number of Caribbean islands and small coastal parts of South America, while Portugal colonised Brazil. By the seventeenth century, Britain had joined in the scramble for the Americas, rivalling Spain in military and economic might. European colonisation of the Americas resulted in successive migratory waves from Europe into the region, as European migrants, especially from the colonising empires, flocked into North and South America in successive droves. In the nineteenth century alone, over fifty million people left Europe for the Americas, contributing to changing the local demography. As more Europeans arrived in the Americas during the fifteenth century, some of them as enslaved persons, new black populations were also migrated to the region from Africa due to transatlantic slavery.

In 1526, the Portuguese completed the first transatlantic slave voyage from Africa to Brazil, followed by shipments to other colonies in the Americas. By the eighteenth century, there was already an overwhelming number of enslaved Africans in the region. From 1770 until 1860, the rate of growth of modern African populations in North America was significantly high, resulting in an upsurge in non-white populations, which had been on the decline as a result of the decimation of the original indigenous populations in the region. More migration in recent periods, starting from the mid-twentieth century, saw more people from other continents arriving and settling in North and South America.

In today's Europe, formerly part of old Eurasia, the founding population consisted of dark-skinned African migrants in the southern region and light-skinned Asian migrants in the northern region. Both groups were joined some centuries later by a fresh batch of Asian migrants who arrived in the southern region, after which the light skin became widely spread across Europe. More migration occurred into Europe, over time, from different parts of Asia and Africa. From about 1200 BC to 146 BC, Phoenicians from The Eastern Mediterranean began to cross over to the European coastland, subsequently expanding across Spain, France, Malta, Greece and Italy. Between 911 to 605 BC, the Assyrian conquest of Cyprus and neighbouring areas, including Armenia, Georgia and Azerbaijan, resulted in the migration from Mesopotamia into Europe. Similarly, Achaemenid (or the First Persian Empire) control of the Thrace—a region in Southeast Europe which includes Bulgaria, Greece and Turkey—between 512 to 343 BC brought with it fresh migrant from Iran into southeastern Europe.

The predominance of population groups of Asian descent in the continent resulted in the Indo-European population category and its subsequent development; significantly, an estimated over two-third (313 of 445) of current Indo-European languages belong to the Indo-Iranian (or Indo-Aryan) branch. It could then be said that Indo-Aryan birthed Indo-European, more or less.

Although the Indo-Aryan population had become significant across Europe by this time, the continent was never wholly Indo-Aryan or Indo-European. People of direct African descent also constituted Europe's overall population, particularly in the south. For instance, some of the ancient Greeks who founded the Minoan civilisation, the first in ancient Greece, which existed around 3000 and 1100 BC, came from Africa. The Mycenaean civilisation, which succeeded Minoan, existed from

1600 to 1100 BC and was founded by a combined population of African and Mediterranean descent. In a similar period, Europe was also home to other non-Indo-European populations. Between 2000 and 1200 BC, the Celts existed in central Europe, east of the Rhine. Greek historian Diodorus Siculus described the hair of these Celts as "thick and shaggy like a horse's mane," suggesting an African rather than Indo-European descent. Ancient Rome, like ancient Greece, was also significantly comprised of a dark African population across the empire. The Roman Empire subsequently dominated Europe, exercising colonial authority over most of the continent, including Britain, Spain, Portugal, and France. Black African populations were significant in most of Roman Europe, notably Britain, Portugal, and Spain, with some of their remnants constituting various ethnic minority indigenous black populations in southern European countries.

Further Indo-Aryan migration from northern Europe aided the predominance of the Indo-European population across Europe; in the second century BC, Germanic people migrated south and east from Scandinavia in Northern Europe, where they had live from as far back as about 1700 BC. While some Germanic people, the Goths, migrated east, settling along the Baltic Sea Coast, others went south along the Rhine river—consequently pushing the resident Celts in the east, west of the Rhine—reaching as far as the Danube region. Another group, Teutones and Cimbri, went further south as far as southern France and northern Italy.

During the Roman Empire period, around 70 AD, Jewish migrants (mostly practitioners of Judaism and some ethnic Israelites) escaped to Europe following various persecutions in

Israel, culminating in the destruction of Jerusalem. By 370 AD, the Huns had arrived on the Volga from central Asia, rapidly expanding westward, as a result pushing many Germanic people into the then western province of the Roman Empire. During the decline of the Roman Empire, beginning around the fourth century AD, widespread migration occurred within and into Europe, mostly into Roman territory. A significant part of this migration involved the Germanic and Hun peoples. A region of western Europe (Gaul), previously under Roman control, witnessed an influx of migrants of Germanic people, the Franks, who established the Frankish kingdom, which became the nucleus of France and Germany. During the same period, another Germanic people, the Burgundians, migrated in large numbers to Northwestern Italy, Switzerland and eastern France from Poland having arrived from the Baltic region many years earlier.

The initial Anglo-Saxon settlement of Britain occurred during the fifth century, following the fall of the Roman Empire. From early-sixth century, Slavs spread to inhabit the majority of Central, Eastern and Southeastern Europe, having originally migrated to Europe from Central and Northern Asia. Magyars (modern-day Hungarians), Khazars and Turkic Pechenegs (both Turkic people) arrived in Europe around the eighth century.

From early in the eighth century onwards, waves of Arab migration into Europe occurred following the conquering of European nations by Arab-Muslims, including Cyprus, Crete, Sicily, Malta, and Greece. During the eighth to tenth centuries, Berbers from North Africa arrived in Southern Europe, establishing a significant presence in Spain and Portugal, where they subsequently exercised dominant control. In the thirteenth century, the Mongol launched an invasion of Europe and with the invasion came waves of Mongol migration into northern Europe. During the fourteenth century, the Ottomans (also known as modern Turkish) crossed into Europe following the conquest of the Balkans by the Ottoman Empire. Between 1250 to 1500 AD, the Romani people arrived in Europe from Asia. As witnessed in North and South America, transatlantic slavery also led to an upsurge in a declining black African population in Europe, especially the south. From the 1450s, the Portuguese transported huge numbers of enslaved people from Africa to Spain, Portugal, Italy, and eventually to countries in Northern Europe. It is important to point out that the black African population in Europe during this period was not exclusively made up of enslaved or formerly enslaved people.

Before enslaved people began to be brought into Europe, there was already a significant black population in the continent, with sizeable numbers in Britain, Spain and Portugal. Black Africans have a significant history in Europe, where they were once a majority, and have continued to impact the continent positively since prehistory. British authors such as Peter Fryers, David Olusoga, and Miranda Kaufmann have written extensively about the history of black people in Britain.

From early in the sixteenth century, European colonisation of Southeast Asia led to successive migratory waves into the continent from Asia. In the same period, when people were being migrated from European colonies in Asia to Africa, as enslaved persons and indentured workers, similar migrations were enforced into Europe. Similarly, during the late-nineteenth and mid-twentieth centuries, the European colonisation of Africa resulted in significant migrations from Africa into Europe, thus boosting existing black populations in the continent. Successive migratory waves also occurred in Europe from the Americas, particularly the Caribbean islands, Asia and Africa, thus resulting in the significant Asian and African populations across the continent. Consequent to its migratory history, Europe has become one of the most diversified continents in the world, with an unrivalled degree of multiculturalism.

Finally, in Africa, where it all began, inward and outward migration also impacted the regional demography. The founding population of Africa did not all migrate outwardly during the early migratory waves. Also, further migration occurred over time both into and out of the continent. Needless to point out, Africa was wholly black initially, remaining so until a more recent period. East Africa is the part of Africa where the oldest human remains were found, leading scholars to suggest it was the part of Africa that humans originated. As early humans travelled out of the continent through the Northeast, subsequent migration took place southwards, perhaps at the same or a later period.

A genetic study reveals that about 130,000 years ago, there were two main ancestral population clusters in Africa: a group consisting of bearers of the mtDNA haplogroup L0 and another consisting of bearers of the L1–6 haplogroup.

The term "haplogroup" is a combination of haplotypes and group. Haplotype refers either to the DNA sequence of a person's mtDNA (which is passed down from a mother to both her male and female children) or the DNA sequence of a person's Y chromosome (which is passed down from a father to only his male children). A group of similar haplotypes that share a common ancestry and are often inherited together is grouped into a haplogroup. Haplogroups are used to establish a direct line of descent.

The Khoisan people in southern Africa are descended from bearers of the L0 haplogroup. The term "Khoisan" is a combination of "Khoikhoi" and "San"—names used to refer to two different indigenous peoples of southern Africa. Khoisan is used as a collective term representing these two population groups, as a catch-all term for the "non-Bantu" indigenous peoples in Africa's South. They are believed to be directly linked to the earliest human ancestors in Africa. The rest of Africa's population during this period (about 130,000 years ago) descended from bearers of the haplogroup L1–6. This haplogroup dominated the central region of Africa at the time. A particular migration—the historic Bantu Expansion—changed Africa's demography more than any other migration in known history.

The Bantu people, comprised of several hundred indigenous groups in sub-Saharan Africa, have their origin in the Niger-Congo Region of Western Africa, particularly the adjoining Cameroon and Nigeria regions. The Bantu expansion supposedly occurred in at least two major waves, between 1000 BC and 1 AD. Linguistic analysis suggests it proceeded in two directions: the first went across the Congo forest region (towards East Africa), the second (and possibly others) went south along the African coast into Gabon and Angola, or inland along the many south-to-north flowing rivers of the Congo River system. It is estimated that the expansion had reached the south of Africa as early as 300 AD. The Bantu incursion into Southern Africa resulted in a drastic population reduction of the Khoisan people, who until then, predominated the region. The remnant of the Khoisan people was displaced and driven into remote areas of the region. Bantu and Khoisan remained the major groups in Southern Africa for several centuries afterwards. The Bantus founded the first known civilisation in the region—Mapungubwe—now part of a National Park in Limpopo Province of South Africa and a UNESCO World Heritage Site, and also the Great Zimbabwe; a medieval city in the South-Eastern hills of Zimbabwe and the capital of the defunct Kingdom of Zimbabwe.

Southern Africa's population remained largely indigenous and predominantly black until the fifteenth century when Europeans began to make contact with the region. European explorers began to arrive in the region, starting with the Portuguese, followed by the Dutch, who arrived at the Cape in 1652 subsequently setting up settlements. The Dutch later brought other migrants from India, Indonesia, Mauritius, and Madagascar to work as slaves for the Dutch East India Company, resulting in the local Asian population. Among these Dutch migrants were settlers of German origin. They were joined in 1688 by French migrants (i.e., Huguenots, an ethnoreligious group of French Protestants who were fleeing religious persecution in France under the Catholic). The British were already present in the Cape before 1795, and by 1805 had colonised it. In 1820, the British authorities persuaded middle-class British people to migrate to South Africa. These European settlers began to venture into the interior of South Africa from the Cape, starting from 1777. After 1806, some Dutch-speaking inhabitants of the Cape Colony trekked inland, first in small groups. Eventually, in the 1830s, larger numbers

migrated in what came to be known as the Great Trek. Following
a succession of internal wars and conflicts, in 1909, the South
Africa Act 1909 consolidated the Cape Colony, Natal, Transvaal,
and Orange Free State into one country as an independent
dominion of the British Empire. This encouraged further
migration from Europe, particularly Britain, resulting in the
expansion of the European population deeper into Southern
Africa, including Zimbabwe, Namibia, and Angola, where few
European settlers already existed. This is how white South
African populations came about.

In Northern Africa, Berbers and Nubians constituted the
major groups for a long period. The Berbers are indigenous to
Northern Africa, having descended from ancestors who inhabited
the Northwestern region of Africa from at least 10000 BC. In
historical times, they expanded south into the Sahara. On the
other hand, the Nubians are descended from the earlier
inhabitants of the central Nile valley. Indigenous peoples from the
Sahara began to move towards the Nile by around 7000 BC,
settling in the central Nile Valley Region. The Nubians unified
several chiefdoms in Upper and Lower Egypt, in around 3100 BC,
to found the First Dynasty of ancient Egypt.

By the eighth century BC, Phoenicians and ancient
Greeks of Indo-European ancestry were already present along
the Mediterranean coasts neighbouring northern Africa. The
Phoenicians developed a great presence in Northern Africa,
establishing colonies from Tripoli (Libya) to the Atlantic while
controlling the Western Mediterranean and most of Northern
Africa, except Egypt, which came under Greek rule following its
conquest by Alexander the Great in 332 BC. In 30 BC, the Roman

presence was established in Northern Africa following Egypt's conquest by Roman Emperor Gaius Octavius. Arab migration into Northern Africa started from about 642 AD, with the first Arab invasion, which advanced as far as Tripoli. Subsequent invasions occurred, from 670 AD onwards, further expanding Arab presence in the region, particularly in Tunisia and Algeria. After the fifteenth century, the Ottoman Empire loosely controlled a vast part of the region, including Algiers, Tunis, and Tripoli, but not Morocco, consequently introducing the Turkish population into the region. By this time, the Berber and Nubian populations, who had become partly admixed with these other groups through interbreeding, became dispersed southwards while some Berbers were also dispersed into the Mediterranean area.

During the eighteenth and nineteenth centuries, the region came under European colonisation as the British, French, Spanish, and Italians made colonies of several countries in the region resulting in a fresh influx of migrants from Europe into Northern Africa.

The Berbers expanded south into the Sahara area in later periods, while the Nubians were displaced and pushed further south down the Nile valley towards its middle region (i.e., part of Sudan). These expansions extended to cover the northern part of East Africa; linguistic analysis point to migration from the middle Nile basin into the African Great Lakes region (in the northern part of East Africa). The southern part was occupied, until the Bantu expansion, by the Khoisan peoples. Most of East Africa was later affected by the Bantu expansion. The Bantu expansion introduced agriculture into much of the African Great Lakes region, subsequently slowly intensifying farming and grazing over all suitable areas in East Africa. This brought local populations in the northern part in contact with Arab and Austronesian-speaking settlers who were already in the southeastern coastal areas.

The population in Eastern Africa was further diversified during the fifteenth century as Europeans came to the region. The Portuguese came first, initially focusing mainly on a coastal strip centred around Mombasa (in Kenya) before extending their presence to Tanzania after 1505 AD. During the seventeenth century, the British, Dutch and Omani Arabs made incursions into the African Great Lakes region resulting in Omani Arab colonisation of Kenyan and Tanzanian coastal areas. In 1839, Omani power in the region was consolidated with the relocation of Omani capital to Zanzibar (in Tanzania). It flourished until 1964, when the Zanzibar Revolution brought an end to Omani rule in the region. Between the nineteenth and twentieth centuries, East Africa became the target of European colonisation, with Britain, France, and Germany as the region's key players. This colonisation resulted in European population groups in East Africa. Although the Asian population already existed in East Africa before the abolition of slavery—some Indian traders had originally followed the Arab trading routes inland on the coast of Kenya and Tanzania—their numbers rose exponentially as a result of this colonisation effort. Asian workers were brought in to replace slave labour, especially for the construction of railway lines. The rise in the Asian population of East Africa was halted during the latter part of the twentieth century. A major factor was the 1972 expulsion of people of Asian descent from Uganda under General Idi Amin's leadership. This led to a significant number of East African Asians leaving the continent and migrating to Europe (notably Britain), while others fled to the USA and Canada. Those who remained in the continent fled to neighbouring countries (e.g., Kenya). It is worth pointing out that in 1992, the Ugandan government facilitated the return to the country of some of those who fled during the expulsion in 1972.

In West Africa, where the Bantus who went on to expand across Africa originated—earlier settlers in the region had arrived by 12000 BC. Stone industries, known as the Stone Age, were found primarily in the Savannah region, where pastoral tribes existed using chiselled stone blades and spears. In the fifth millennium BC, the ancestors of the Mandé peoples began entering the area as the development of sedentary farming began to take place in the region. Evidence of domesticated cattle has been found for this period, along with limited cereal crops. In the third millennium BC, a major migration of Sahel cattle farmers occurred, thereby bringing these pastoralists from Northern Africa in contact with the developed hunter-gatherers of the Guinea region in West Africa. Archaeology shows evidence of sizeable urban populations in West Africa beginning in the second millennium BC, where symbiotic trade relations existed long before the trans-Saharan trade began.

By 1500 BC, the West African people associated with the Nok culture already existed in Northern Nigeria. Around the first millennium BC, the Bantu expansion began. As the Bantus radiated across the continent, other groups emerged while existing ones thrived and advanced, among whom are the Djenné-Djenno people (located in the Niger River Valley in Mali), Serer people (from the old Senegambia, which includes Senegal,

The Gambia, Guinea-Bissau, and parts of Mauritania, Mali and Guinea) and the Sahelian Kingdoms. The Sahelian kingdoms included: The ancient Ghana Empire (founded as early as the seventh century by a branch of the Mandé people), Mali Empire (founded in the thirteenth century, also by Mandé people), Songhai Empire (founded around the ninth century by the Songhai people who descended from fishermen on the Middle Niger River), and the Sokoto Caliphate founded by Fulani people who had originally moved from Mauritania first settling in Futa Tooro (along the borders of Senegal and Mauritania) and then Futa Djallon (in the centre of Guinea), and subsequently throughout the rest of West Africa.

Although the people of West Africa had by 400 BC already made contact with some Mediterranean people present in Saharan Africa, the trade relationship which existed initially was fairly small. By the late eighth century, however, this Mediterranean presence had increased significantly, and Islam introduced in the region. For instance, the Ghana Empire was at a time administered by a combination of Berber Muslim-administrators and the *Ghana* (or King) from the indigenous people. In the tenth century, Islam was steadily growing in the region, and by 1492, a Muslim kingdom, Askiya Dynasty, was founded. Successive historical periods saw the emergence of other population groups in the region, one of whom were the Akan people who initially settled in the Sahel having come from Central Africa before subsequently migrating to the West. The Akan people settled in an area covering Ghana and Ivory Coast. By the twelfth century, they had established the Kingdom of Bonoman. Others include: the Aja people who inhabit the Southwest of Benin Republic and the Southeast of Togo and founded the Dahomey Kingdom in the early seventeenth century. The Yoruba people who founded the Oyo Empire in the sixteenth century (Note that the first empire founded by the Yoruba was at Ile-Ife). The Edo people who founded the Benin Empire in the mid-fifteenth century. The Igbo people in Southeastern Nigeria who founded the Kingdom of Nri in the tenth century.

Europeans arrived in Western Africa during the fifteenth century. The Portuguese came first in 1445 and established a trading post at Arguin Island off the coast of Senegal. By 1475, Portuguese traders had reached as far as the Bight of Benin in the Gulf of Guinea on the western African coast. Transatlantic slave trade began almost immediately after, resulting in enforced mass migration from West Africa (and other parts of Africa) to Europe and the Americas. Transatlantic slavery was shortly followed by European colonisation, which began in the 1880s with the Scramble for Africa, resulting in European settlements in the region. However, this did not result in any tangible local European population in western Africa except for mixed groups derived from interbreeding. Late in the twentieth century, migrants from China began to move in huge numbers to different parts of Africa.

The foregoing represents a highly summarised historical timeline of different global migrations that have significantly impacted the regional demography of the different continents. It also highlights how various indigenous populations became displaced and reduced to a minority, in some cases, due to mass migration from other continents involving migrants of different ethnicities. This shows how almost every local population of the different regions and sub-regions of the world is a product of migrations, meaning that we are all migrants regardless of whatever part of the world we have recently originated from.

CHAPTER THREE

African

Civilisations

The true story of Africa has remained largely untold until date, while incompleteness, inaccuracy, deliberate distortion, and bias characterise popular rendition and narrative of the history of Africa and that of her various peoples. Not a few people, for instance, are unaware that Africa is the place where humans originated or that civilisation first began in Africa from where it spread across the world. The popular face of Africa today is one defined by poverty, hunger, diseases, and primitiveness. It is instructive to note that this deplorable image of Africa and her people is not only inaccurate but also intentional because Africa needs to be represented as underprivileged and needy to make her exploitation possible, easy, and justifiable.

Many aspects of Africa's history have deliberately been hidden by those who took it upon themselves to write her story, and for very good reason: knowledge is power, and information is invaluable. And so, to ensure that Africa and her people remain under exploitative control and manipulation, internally and externally, disinformation is a vital necessity. Hence, Africa is represented as it is now and has been for many centuries.

Interestingly, this has not always been the case as Africa was once renowned for her wealth and greatness and was at a time in history a global centre of attraction for the acquisition of knowledge and tourism. For instance, many of the most important ancient Greek scholars: Thales, Solon, Plato, and, Eudoxus, were schooled in ancient Egypt when Nubian Dynasties still ruled it.

Nubians, some of whose descendants can be found today in southern Sudan, unified Upper and Lower Egypt founding the Early Dynastic Period and ruled over Egypt until c. 1650 BC when the Fifteenth Dynasty was founded by the Hyksos—a people of West Asian descent and the first non-black rulers of Egypt. The great sixteenth-century champion of Copernicus, Giordano Bruno, wrote: "We Greeks own Egypt, the grand monarchy of letters and nobility, to be the parent of our fables, metaphors and doctrines." Africa remained a global attraction in later historical periods, attracting visitors from across the world, including Europe and Asia. During the thirteenth century, the city of Timbuktu in ancient Mali was home to a thriving civilisation with established trade links with Europe and Asia, which attracted tourists from different parts of the world. An African king, Abu Bakr II, a fourteenth-century Mansa (King) of the Mali Empire, had conducted an audacious voyage to the Americas in 1311, arriving in Brazil, almost two hundred years before Christopher Columbus landed in the Caribbean in 1492.

Africa's fortune and place in history began to decline following contact with explorers from Europe during the fifteenth century, but not immediately. Some earlier Europeans who explored Africa from the fifteenth century gave a positive review of the continent and people they encountered during their travels. Scottish explorer, Mungo Park— famous for "discovering" the Niger river—had travelled to West Africa in 1795 under the sponsorship of the African Association, a London-based club dedicated to the exploration of West Africa, for the primary purpose of discovering the origin and course of the River Niger and also the location of Timbuktu—the "lost city" of gold. He travelled from Portsmouth, England, in May 1795, arriving at the River Gambia by June, reaching the River Niger, at Ségou (Mali), by July 1796 after escaping a four-month imprisonment in the hands of a local chief. Park was the first European to travel this far into West Africa. In his book, *Travels in the Interior Districts of Africa*, which was first published in 1799, he writes: "Whatever difference there is between the negro and European, in the conformation of the nose, and the colour of the skin, there is none in the genuine sympathies and characteristic feelings of our common nature." Upon encountering a group of Africans who were recently abducted and being transported into slavery while travelling through Mali, he writes: "They were all very inquisitive, but they viewed me at first with looks of horror, and repeatedly asked if my countrymen were cannibals...A deeply-rooted idea that the whites purchase Negroes for the purpose of devouring them, or of selling them on to others that they may be devoured hereafter, naturally makes the slaves contemplate a journey towards the coast with great terror, insomuch that the *Slatees* [Black slave merchants] are forced to keep them constantly in irons, and watch them very closely, to prevent their escape." This depiction of the Africans observed by Park, based on firsthand experience, contradicts the later representation of Africans as "savages and cannibals" by other historians of European descent.

Instructively, transatlantic slavery and the subsequent colonisation of Africa occasioned the change in attitude towards Africa and her peoples. In an attempt to justify the inhumanity of this particular instance of slavery and the exploitation of the continent through colonisation, Africa and Africans needed to be misrepresented as a different and inferior "race" and primitive people in need of rescue from self-destruction by Europeans through western civilisation. Consequently, historians of European descent embarked on a concerted campaign of rewriting history in their favour at the expense of the people whose story was being rewritten, leading to the destruction of a huge wealth of historical records about Africa's history and the distortion of most of the information about Africa which survived. Suffice it to say that a more significant part of the history taught under the system of western education is aimed at disinformation and therefore cannot and should not be relied upon as a credible source of information relating to history, particularly that of Africa.

The extent of this distortion is such that even the size of Africa had to be deliberately reduced in the popular maps in current circulation around the world. Most maps in circulation are based on the Mercator Projection named after Flemish cartographer Gerardus Mercator who invented it in 1569. This projection shrinks the size of Africa on the map while greatly exaggerating that of Europe, Greenland, and Antarctica. The reason given for this was that it was done for the purpose of navigation. Thus, the enlargement of the sizes of Europe, Greenland, and Antarctica was to enable cartographers plot the actual location of cities and routes in the Northern Hemisphere frequented by European explorers, thereby leaving Africa shrunk in size in comparison. There is, however, a different view on this, with some scholars arguing that the misrepresentation in size was politically motivated and aimed at "enhancing the size of Western states, vis-à-vis power of representation and representation of power, as a useful tool for imperialism and colonialism." Interestingly, a more recent and advanced projection, the Gall-Peters Projection, originally invented in 1855 by James Gall and made more popular in the early 1970s by Arno Peters, an equal-area projection based on the scale sizes which represents a more accurate size of Africa in relation to the other continents (see Fig 1a), had been ignored by popular mapmakers until very recently. Maps using the Gall-Peters projection are now widely in use in schools in Britain and some states in the US and are being promoted by UNESCO. The Gall-Peters Projection places Africa more centrally on the world map and presents it as the biggest continent in the world—about three times bigger than Canada! To understand Africa's true history, we will need to explore stories presently hidden, most likely through deliberate exclusion, from the official and popular history in current circulation.

Hidden History

The true history of Africa and the African people is told by historians of African descent. Oral history is an integral part of the tradition in Africa, with her history preserved from generation to generation through storytelling by local historians, known in parts of western Africa as griots (also *jali* or *jeli*), who are the repositories of local history and tradition. These local historians themselves would have been the primary source of local history for their European counterparts, whose version became popular and enshrined in world history, howbeit a heavily distorted version of history which had been corrupted through various losses in translation, as well as intentionally in some cases.

A significant part of Africa's history before records began is relatively unknown. However, archaeological studies have yielded some important and interesting discoveries revealing the extent of technological advancement in Africa in prehistoric periods. For instance, the Oldowan technology, the earliest stone industry in prehistory, is now known to have originated in Africa, from where it spread to Asia and subsequently Europe. Oldowan tools were first used to scavenge kills made by other predators and to harvest carrion and marrow from their bones. It was succeeded by the Acheulean technology many centuries later. Archaeology has also revealed that the art of making fire by striking stone objects together also originated in the continent before the First Wave of migration. Also, it is now known that prehistoric Africa birthed astronomy and mathematics: the earliest form of a lunar calendar was found inscribed on a bone—the Ishango bone—which was discovered in the Congo Basin region. The bone, dated between 23000 and 18000 BC, was discovered in 1960 by Belgian geologist Jean de Heinzelin de Braucourt in Ishango, in the Democratic Republic of the Congo (DRC)—The Ishango bone is now on permanent exhibition at the Royal Belgian Institute of Natural Sciences in Brussels. The etchings on the bone are in three columns with marks asymmetrically grouped into sets, with the third column interpreted as a table of prime numbers. The etchings have been variously interpreted by scholars as a prehistoric calculator and lunar calendar. Similarly, megaliths found at Nabta Playa, once a large internally drained basin in the Nubian Desert (located in Egypt), are examples of the world's first known archaeoastronomical device. It is noteworthy that the Nabta Playa megaliths predate Stonehenge (in Wiltshire, England) by some thousand years.

Agriculture and other agro-related activities similarly existed in prehistoric Africa: By around 16000 BC, from the Red Sea Hills to the northern Ethiopian Highlands, nuts, grasses, and tubers were being collected for food. Between 13000 and 11000 BC, people in this region began collecting wild grains, a practice that subsequently spread to Western Asia. Between 10000 and 8000 BC, Northeastern Africa was cultivating wheat and barley and engaged in raising sheep and cattle from Southwestern Asia. In the steppes and savannahs of the Sahara and Sahel in Northern West Africa, between 8000 and 6000 BC, the Mandé people started to collect and domesticate wild millet, local rice species, and sorghum; and later, gourds, watermelons, castor beans, and cotton. They also started capturing wild cattle held in circular thorn hedges, thus resulting in their domestication. Likewise, they made pottery, built stone settlements, and engaged in fishing using bone-tipped harpoons, which became a major activity in local streams and lakes. The Mandé have been credited with the independent development of agriculture in West Africa starting from about 3000 to 4000 BC. In West Africa, between 9000 and 5000 BC, Niger-Congo peoples domesticated the oil palm, raffia palm, black-eyed peas, indigenous species of groundnuts, okra, and kola nuts. They invented polished stone axes for clearing forests since most of the plants grew in the forest.

Most of Southern Africa was occupied by the Pygmy and Khoisan peoples, who were hunter-gatherers and who produced some of the oldest rock art. Just prior to the desertification of the Sahara, the communities which developed south of Egypt were full participants in the Neolithic revolution (or First Agricultural Revolution) and lived a settled to semi-nomadic lifestyle with domesticated plants and animals. In Central Africa, artefacts dating back to over 100,000 years have been discovered, while extensive walled sites and settlements, dated to 1000 BC, have recently been found in Zilum, Chad. By around 1000 BC, Bantu migrants had reached the Great Lakes Region in Central Africa, subsequently settling as far as Angola halfway through that millennium. Trade and improved agricultural techniques supported more sophisticated societies giving rise to early civilisations such as Sao, Kanem, Bornu, Shilluk, Baguirmi, and Wadai. By 1000 BC, iron working had been introduced in

Northwestern Africa. However, there is archaeological evidence of iron-smelting in the modern-day Central African Republic and Cameroon with a possible date of 3000 to 2500 BC. Iron smelting was developed in the area between Lake Chad and the African Great Lakes between 1000 and 600 BC, long before it reached ancient Egypt. The first metals to be smelted in Africa took place in 4000 BC and included lead, copper, and bronze. Metal working in West Africa is dated to as early as 2500 BC at Egaro, west of the Termit in Niger; iron working was practiced there by 1500 BC. Before 500 BC, the Nok culture in the Jos Plateau, in central Nigeria, was already smelting iron.

The foregoing represents a highly summarised outline of some key aspects of Africa's history in prehistoric periods. Another summarised outline of important aspects of Africa's hidden history is now presented on a regional basis.

NORTHERN AFRICA

Ancient Egypt is unarguably the most prominent African civilisation known all over the world. It is widely acknowledged as the "Cradle of Civilisation" and has the enviable reputation of being responsible for other historic civilisations across the world, including those of ancient Greece and Rome. The first dynasty in ancient Egypt was founded by Nubians, descendants of the earlier inhabitants of the central Nile valley, a region previously referred to as Nubia, a people famous for their skill and precision with bows and arrows. The desertification of the Sahara led to settlements being concentrated in the Nile Valley area, subsequently leading to the emergence of various sacral chiefdoms. The Nile Delta region of Lower Egypt, Upper Egypt, and parts of the Nile in Nubia experienced the largest population pressure, thereby necessitating regulation. Bureaucracies were formed consequent to the rapid proliferation of chiefdoms; the first and most powerful was Ta-Seti. Several sacral chiefdoms also emerged across Upper and Lower Egypt. By about 3600 BC, societies along the Nile had based their culture on raising crops and the domestication of animals. Shortly after 3600 BC, they had begun to grow and advance rapidly towards refined civilisation. For instance, the extensive use of copper became common during this period, and the Mesopotamian process of sun-dried bricks and architectural building principles also became popular. During this period, the Egyptian writing system was further developed; what initially comprised only a few symbols would increase to more than two hundred symbols, both phonograms and ideograms. In 3100 BC, Narmer, who is believed to have ruled as Pharaoh Menes, unified the different chiefdoms into a single political entity, thus establishing the Early Dynastic Period of ancient Egypt, which lasted till about 2686 BC. The Early Dynastic Period was succeeded by what eighteenth-century historians referred to as the Old Kingdom. This reference is more of a superficial distinction because, not only was the last king of the former period related to the first two kings of the latter period, the capital (the royal residence) also remained the same (what would later be known as Memphis). The Old Kingdom also referred to as the "Age of the Pyramids," spanned the period between c. 2686–2181 BC and comprised the Third to Sixth dynasties. This period witnessed a revolutionary change in Egyptian architecture, including the art of pyramid-building and large-scale building projects. The Old Kingdom was succeeded by the First Intermediate Period (often referred to as a "dark period" in ancient Egyptian history), which lasted between c. 2181–2055 BC, and comprised the Seventh to Eleventh dynasties. It was a dynamic historical period during which the rule of Egypt was roughly divided between two competing power bases—one each in Lower and Upper Egypt. This period ended with the reunification of Egypt, under Mentuhotep II, during the second part of the Eleventh dynasty, marking the beginning of the Middle Kingdom. The Middle Kingdom lasted between c. 2050–1710 BC, and comprised part of the Eleventh to part of the Thirteenth dynasties. Instructively, Egypt up to this period was predominantly black—Nubian. The Twelfth dynasty ended towards the end of the nineteenth century BC, following the death of Queen Sobekneferu, and was succeeded by a much weaker Thirteenth dynasty notable for the accession of the first formally recognised Semitic-speaking king, Khendjer. The Thirteenth dynasty proved unable to hold on to the whole of ancient Egypt, resulting in a provincial ruling family of Western Asian descent in Avaris, in the marshes of the eastern Nile Delta, breaking away from the central authority to form the Fourteenth dynasty.

The Middle Kingdom was followed by the Second Intermediate Period, during which the Hyksos dynasty emerged in Egypt. The Hyksos people originally came from Western Asia and were relatively lighter skinned than the Nubians. They established the Fifteenth dynasty in Egypt following their conquest of Thebes, the capital of the Middle Kingdom, in c. 1650 BC. Hyksos reign in Egypt lasted between c. 1650–1550 BC. The

Second Intermediate Period was succeeded by the New Kingdom, which comprised the Eighteenth to Twentieth dynasties, and existed between c. 1550–1077 BC. This was the period when Egyptian kings began to rule as Pharaohs. It is believed to be ancient Egypt's most prosperous period and the peak of its power, the time it attained its greatest territorial extent. The New Kingdom was followed by another intermediate period—the Third Intermediate Period—which began following the death of Ramesses XI and lasted between c.1069–664 BC. The disintegration of the New Kingdom encouraged the reassertion of the Nubian independence, subsequently leading to the establishment of the Twenty-fifth dynasty, founded by Nubians. The Twenty-fifth dynasty was subsequently defeated by an Assyrian invasion that employed the use of iron weapons, which until then was unknown in the whole of Egypt. The Nubians were eventually pushed further down the Nile River, where they settled in an area that includes today's Sudan.

They established the Kingdom of Kush in the area in c. 785 BC, during the New Kingdom period in Egypt, which existed till c. 350 AD. The kingdom had its capital initially at Napata (or today's Karima) before moving to Meroë in c. 591 BC. This region was known in early Greek geography as Aethiopia. In Egypt, the Assyrians were also later ousted by Persians, who in 525 BC founded the Twenty-sixth dynasty. The Third Intermediate Period was followed by the Late Period, which existed between c. 664–332 BC, ending with the conquest of the Persian Empire in 305 BC by Greek emperor Alexander the Great, following which the Ptolemic dynasty was established. The last ruler of Ptolemic Egypt was Cleopatra VII, whose death, coupled with a Roman conquest in 30 BC, resulted in Roman rule in Egypt.

The Berbers were another founding and dominant group in northern Africa apart from the Nubians. They occupied the region west of the Nile to Egypt, extending into the Mediterranean and, in a later period, the Niger River in West Africa. They are believed to have inhabited the Maghreb in Northwestern Africa from at least 10000 BC and made contact with other peoples in the Mediterranean area in prehistoric periods, particularly the Phoenicians with whom they often had asymmetrical interactions. In 814 BC, the city of Carthage in Tunisia was established by Phoenicians from Tyre, Lebanon. By 600 B, Carthage had become a major trading and political entity in the region and had also gained its independence from the Phoenician state of Tyre, thus becoming an empire. The Carthaginian Empire consisted of Phoenician city-states across northern Africa. At its height, its territory included most of the western Mediterranean, including Spain. The empire was a contemporary of the Roman Republic with whom it fought a series of wars; The Punic Wars: First Punic War (264–241 BC), Second Punic War (218–201 BC), and Third Punic War (149–146 BC). Notably, Carthaginian general Hannibal is regarded as one of the greatest military minds in history. After the third and final Punic War, Carthage was destroyed, and the empire fell into Roman hands.

The fall of Carthage is very significant in Africa and world history for two main reasons: firstly, it led to Roman expansion into Africa, following which Rome shifted from regional to global imperialism, thus laying the foundation for the global domination which would be pursued by successive nation-states, particularly in Europe, and which continues today. Secondly, Rome's control of Carthage and subsequently of Egypt shifted the stream of civilisation development from Africa to Europe. Much of what Africa had to offer was thus assimilated into the Roman intellectual legacy as a result. This period represents a watershed in Africa's history because it was from this time onwards that Africa's civilisation began to crumble, having been hijacked by Rome, eventually culminating in its total or near extinction. Significantly, this period also marks the origins of what would later culminate in the so-called Western Civilisation.

Although Carthage was founded and controlled by Phoenicians during the empire era, it was part of Berber indigenous territory. Its prosperity around 500 BC fostered the growth of indigenous Berber kingdoms. Two of such kingdoms—Numidia and Mauretania—emerged as independent nation-states during the third century BC due to a weakened Carthaginian empire following the Punic Wars. The Kingdom of Numidia existed between c. 202–40 BC and comprised of Algeria and parts of Tunisia and Libya. An interesting fact about the Kingdom of Mauretania is that it was established by the Mauri people, of Berber ancestry, from whom the historic Moors would derive their name. Legend has it that it was once ruled by King Atlas, who is credited with inventing the celestial globe. Both kingdoms came under the Roman influence when Carthage fell. The Romans were themselves conquered in Northern Africa in c. 420 AD, by the Vandals, a Germanic people. The Romans later reconquered the region in c. 534 AD. A Muslim conquest subsequently ensued between 647–709 AD, during which most of the region was ruled by the Arab-Muslim Umayyad Caliphate which was succeeded, in 969 AD, by the Fatimid dynasty.

Between the tenth and thirteenth centuries, nomadic Arabs, known as Bedouins, mass-migrated out of the Arabian Peninsula into the region.

This movement is historically significant because it led to the spread of the Arabic language in Northern Africa while also hastening the decline of the native Berber languages, and the Arabisation of the region.

The fifteenth-century witnessed the reconquering of Northern Africa by the Europeans, starting with Portugal around 1415. A few centuries later, Spain and Portugal had acquired ports on the northern coasts of Africa, notably Tangiers, Tripoli, and Tunis. These were subsequently taken over by the Ottoman Empire, which eventually lost Morocco to the Arab Saadi dynasty during the sixteenth century. The Mamluk dynasty retook Egypt from the Ottoman during the seventeenth and eighteenth

centuries as the struggle for control in the region continued. In 1798, French leader Napoleon Bonaparte took control of Egypt but was ousted in 1801 by a joint Ottoman-British coalition force.

The Horn of Africa, in the north of Africa, also boasted of prominent civilisations in times past. The earliest known prehistoric state in the region, known as D'mt, existed during the tenth to fifth centuries BC and was located in an area that included today's Eritrea and Northern Ethiopia. Few records about and by the kingdom survived, this coupled with little archaeological study makes it unclear whether or not it had ended before the later kingdom of Aksum began its early stages of development. Or if it was part of the smaller states united later to form Aksum. The kingdom of D'mt developed irrigation schemes, used ploughs, grew millet, and made iron tools and weapons. The Kingdom of Aksum (or Axum) arose in the region in the first century, existing between c. 100–940 AD, and had powerful emperors who styled themselves as king of kings. It was a major commercial route between Rome and Old India and was regarded as one of the four great powers of her time alongside Persia, Rome, and China. Her rulers minted Aksumite currency, used to facilitate trade, and erected a number of monumental stelae that served a religious purpose in pre-Christian times, one of which at 90 feet is the largest of such structure in the world.

Tradition claims Aksum as the alleged resting place of the biblical Ark of the Covenant (see Exodus 25). It is also believed to be the home of the legendary Queen of Sheba.

It was succeeded by a collection of splinter empire-states: Medri Bahri, Zagwe, Makuria, Alodia, and Sassanid. The Zagwe dynasty existed between c. 900–1270 AD and was succeeded by the Solomonic dynasty. The Ethiopian Empire (also known as Abyssinia) began with the establishment of the Solomonic dynasty from c. 1270, by a lineage who claimed to be descended from King Solomon of Israel. It lasted until 1974 but was briefly under Italian control between 1936 and 1941. An interesting bit of history is that the Ethiopian empire and Liberia were the two political entities in Africa to remain independent during the colonisation of Africa. The Ethiopian Empire was one of the founding members of the United Nations in 1945. The historic

Emperor Haile Selassie was her last ruler before he was deposed in 1974.

Along the Horn of Africa also existed the Somali city-states during the eight and fifth centuries BC, notable among them were Mossylon, Malao, Mundus, and Tabae. These engaged in a lucrative trade network connecting Somali merchants with Phoenicia, Ptolemic Egypt, Greece, Parthian Persia, and the Roman Empire. The Sultanate of Mogadishu (or Kingdom of Magadazo) rose as one of the prominent powers in this region during the tenth century, but is believed to have existed from around the ninth century up to the thirteenth century. It was a trading kingdom centred in modern-day Southern Somalia. The kingdom maintained a vast trading network, dominated the regional gold trade, minted its own currency, and left an extensive architectural legacy. The kingdom was succeeded in the thirteenth century by the Ajuran Sultanate (or Ajuran Empire), which united Mogadishu with other coastal and mainland Somali cities in Southern Somalia and Eastern Ethiopia under a single kingdom.

Moroccan explorer and scholar Ibn Battuta, who travelled to the Somali coast in 1331, described Mogadishu as "an exceedingly large city" with many wealthy merchants. Mogadishu was also noted as a massive metropolis. The Ajuran Empire established diplomatic ties with ancient China, creating the first-ever recorded African community in China. The most notable Somali ambassador in ancient China was known as Sa'id of Mogadishu. In the thirteenth century, the Ajuran Empire was the only hydraulic empire in Africa, using hydraulic engineering to construct many limestone wells and cisterns, some of which are still functional.

The Sultanate of Geledi ruled parts of the Horn of Africa, starting from the late seventeenth century, having defeated various vassal-states of the predecessor Ajuran Empire, which was already in decline. The sultanate was eventually incorporated into Italian Somaliland in 1908. It ended in 1910 with the death of Osman Ahmed, its last Sultan.

EASTERN AFRICA

One of the earliest known indigenous civilisations in Eastern Africa is the Urewe Civilisation which developed and spread in and around the Lake Victoria region. The Urewe culture, which existed from the fifth century BC to the sixth century AD, extended from the Kagera region of Tanzania to as far west as the Kivu region of the Democratic Republic of the Congo, as far east as the Nyanza and western provinces of Kenya, and extending northwards into Uganda, Rwanda, and Burundi. Linguistic studies indicate the culture could have originated from a branch of the first wave of Bantu migrants to settle in Eastern Africa. Urewe culture is easily recognisable through its distinctive, stylish earthenware and highly technical and sophisticated iron-working techniques.

The Empire of Kitara, also known as Kingdom of the Bakitara, was the earliest prominent kingdom to rise in the Great Lakes of Africa area, which at her peak, stretched throughout the Nile Valley and beyond, including Uganda, Northern Tanzania, Eastern Democratic Republic of Congo, Rwanda, Burundi, Zambia, and Malawi. The empire had fragmented into various autonomous states towards the 1300s, giving rise to successive splinter kingdoms. Some powerful kingdoms later arose from the empire. Kingdoms such as the Kingdom of Buganda, which was founded in the late fourteenth century when the kabaka (or ruler) of the Ganda people, Kabaka Kato Kintu, came to exercise solid and centralised control over a unified territory called Buganda in today's Uganda (the name "Uganda" is the Swahili term for Buganda). It had become the largest and most powerful kingdom in the region by the nineteenth century, later becoming part of the British Uganda Protectorate in 1894. The kingdom was given considerable autonomy following Uganda's independence in 1962, including being accorded special federal status within the new nation. However, it was abolished in 1967 due to political conflict between her ruler and the prime minister of Uganda, Milton Obote. The kingdom was, however, restored in 1993.

Another powerful kingdom in the region was the Kingdom of Rwanda which rose to prominence during the seventeenth century but was abolished during the Rwandan Revolution, which occurred from 1959 to 1961. And also, the Kingdom of Burundi which was created in the seventeenth century and remained preserved under colonial rule before later becoming a republic in 1966.

WESTERN AFRICA

Archaeology has shown that sizeable urban populations existed in the western Sahel beginning in the second millennium BC. During this period, technology had advanced in Western Africa represented in the iron industry in the region, which by 1200 BC was highly advanced and included the smelting and forging of tools and weapons. The western region of Africa was notable for her wealth of mineral resources, especially gold, with Timbuktu in ancient Mali widely known as the "City of Gold." Commerce in the region was also highly advanced such that by 400 BC, trading links had been established between the region and the Mediterranean as local merchants traded gold, cotton, metal, and leather in exchange for copper, horses, salt, textiles, and beads. A prominent civilisation—Nok Civilisation —existed in the region in the northern part of today's Nigeria in c. 1500 BC. Nok art which had remained unmoved was recovered from two archaeological sites in the area—Samun Dukiya and Taruga. Radiocarbon and thermos-luminescence tests dated the sculptures to a range of dates between c. 2,900 and 2,000 years ago, making them some of the oldest in Western Africa. The region is also home to the Serer people who lived in the Senegal River valley area and founded the Serer kingdoms, prominent among which are the Kingdom of Sine and the Kingdom of Saloum. Both kingdoms survived till the twentieth century.

Perhaps the most famous and historical kingdoms in Western Africa belong to the kingdoms, which existed in the Sahel—the Sahelian kingdoms. The Sahelian kingdoms were a series of centralised kingdoms in the Sahel which existed from the eighth century to the nineteenth. These kingdoms were very influential within and outside the region; their wealth came from controlling the trade routes across the desert. Their power came from having large pack animals such as camels and horses that were fast enough to keep a large empire under central control and also be useful in battle. All of these kingdoms were also quite decentralised with member states exercising a great deal of autonomy. Of these kingdoms, the Kingdom of Ghana (also the Ghana Empire) was the first to emerge in the region. The Ghana kingdom was originally known by its Soninke name "Ouagadou" before subsequently being referred to by the title of its rulers, "Ghana" (or Ga'na). It rose around the eight century, was centred in today's Mauritania and Senegal, and had a territory which stretched to include the western part of today's Mali. It was first mentioned in writing in 830 AD by Persian scholar Muhammad ibn Musa al-Khwarizmi. In the eleventh century, Arab-born Cordoban scholar Al-Bakri, having travelled to the empire, described it as being able to "put 200,000 men into the field, more than 40,000 of them archers." Al-Bakri also noted that the empire had cavalry units. Ghana Empire was very wealthy, cosmopolitan, and a major trading centre and route in Trans-Saharan Trade. A significant portion of her wealth came from taxes levied on goods that passed through her territory. Ghana Empire thrived until the thirteenth century when it fell. With its fall in c. 1240, her territory became incorporated as part of the Mali Empire, which succeeded her as the dominant power in the area. The legendary King Sundiata Keita founded the Mali Empire in c. 1235. It was one of the largest empires in West African history, spanning from the Atlantic Coast to central parts of the Sahara, at its peak. Mali Empire profoundly influenced the culture of West Africa by spreading its languages, laws, and customs. The most famous ruler of the Malian empire was Musa Keita (also Mansa Musa or Musa I), whose wealth was legendary. He succeeded his brother Abu Bakr II (also spelt Abubakari) in 1311 when the latter handed over power to him in order to pursue knowledge and discovery.

Mansa Abu Bakr II, who ruled Mali in the fourteenth century, had wanted to discover whether the Atlantic Ocean, like the Niger River, had another "bank." His adventure took him to the Americas, when he landed on Recife (a coast in today's Brazil) in 1312, about two hundred years before Christopher Columbus got to the Americas. The griots who revealed this history report that the king made this voyage in a convoy of boats manufactured in the area.

Mali Empire was succeeded by the Songhai Empire, which exercised dominant influence in the region during the fifteenth and sixteenth centuries. The empire, known as the most powerful of the Sahelian kingdoms, rose to prominence under Sonni Ali during the fifteenth century, although a Songhai state had existed since the eleventh century. It was ruled by two main dynasties—the founding Sonni dynasty (c. 1464–1493) and the Askia dynasty (1493–1591). A Moroccan invasion in 1591 saw the collapse of Songhai, which more or less became extinct as an empire after that, although Songhai culture and society persisted in the less powerful Dendi Kingdom, which succeeded it. Dendi was also conquered by the French in 1901 during the period of European colonisation in Africa.

In the Lake Chad area, the Kanem Empire existed from the ninth century, founded by the Sef dynasty, and had its first capital at Njimi (northeast of Lake Chad). Due to its location, it served as a point of contact in trade between North Africa, the Nile Valley, and the sub-Sahara region. In the late fourteenth century, the Sef were forced to abandon Kanem leading to the capital being moved to Birni Ngazargamu (in Bornu, west of Lake Chad). From then, it existed as an independent Bornu Empire. It later recaptured Kanem in the early sixteenth century but retained its capital at Bornu, thus becoming known as the Kanem-Bornu Empire. At its height, it encompassed most of the Chad, Fezzan (i.e. Southern Libya), and today's eastern Niger, Northeastern Nigeria and Northeastern Cameroon. At the beginning of the nineteenth century, the Fulani people (of today's Nigeria) disputed Bornu's suzerainty over the Hausa states to the west of Lake Chad. The conflicts that ensued greatly weakened the empire that died out in 1846, never re-establishing its power. Hausaland took shape as a political and cultural region during the first millennium, in the area between the Niger River and Lake Chad, as a result of the westward expansion of the Hausa peoples. The Hausas founded a collection of states which later became known as Hausa city-states (or Hausa Kingdom) which rose to prominence in the region in the mid-fourteenth century. The seven true Hausa states, or "Hausa Bakwai" are: Biram, Daura, Gobir, Kano, Katsina, Rano, and Zaria and their seven outlying satellites, or "Banza Bakwai"—Zamfara, Kebi, Yauri, Gwari, Nupe, Kororofa, and Yoruba—had no central authority but each existed as an independent city-state instead. By the fourteenth century, Kano had become the most powerful city-state in the Hausa kingdom, having become the base for the trans-Saharan trade in salt, cloth, leather, and grain. By the fifteenth century, the Hausa Kingdom had vibrant trading centres competing with Kanem-Bornu and Mali empires. Her success was cut short by the Fulani people who conquered the kingdom after successive attacks between 1804 and 1808, led by Usman dan Fodio, resulting in the Sokoto Caliphate. The Sokoto Caliphate was a loose confederation of emirates that recognised the suzerainty of the sultan. At its peak, the Sokoto Caliphate linked over thirty different emirates and over ten million people in the most powerful state in its region. It was also one of the most significant empires in Africa in the nineteenth century. It lasted until 1903, when the British absorbed her into the Northern Nigeria Protectorate during colonisation.

Along the Atlantic coast of West Africa existed some very flamboyant indigenous civilisations, empires, or kingdoms. The Kwa-speaking Akan people, originally from East or Central Africa, founded the Kingdom of Bonoman around the twelfth century as a trading state in the area of today's Southern Ghana and Eastern Ivory Coast. The kingdom is widely accepted as the origin of the subgroups of Akan people who migrated outwards at various times in search of gold, consequently establishing new Akan kingdoms in the region. Gold trade, which started to boom in Bonoman as early as in the twelfth century, was the genesis of Akan power and wealth in the region. During the thirteenth century, with the decline of gold in Mali Empire, Bonoman and other Akan kingdoms rose to prominence as key players in the gold trade. Bonoman and other Akan kingdoms (e.g., Denkyira, Akyem, and Akwamu) preceded the historic and very powerful Ashanti Empire (also Asante), which lasted between 1670 and 1957. The Ashanti Empire was established by the Ashanti king, Osei Tutu, late in the seventeenth century. The Golden Stool of Asante served as a sole unifying symbol. Ashanti Empire eventually expanded to cover most of modern-day Ghana. Due to its military prowess, wealth, architecture, sophisticated hierarchy and culture, the empire has been extensively studied and has more historiographies by European historians than any other indigenous culture of sub-Saharan Africa. It remained powerful for most of the nineteenth century but was later reduced to a very weakened state following the British conquest in the five Anglo-Ashanti wars, which ended in 1901. The region also saw the rise of the Dahomey Kingdom early in the seventeenth century, founded by the Aja people (of today's Benin Republic). It was a powerful centralised state with an organised domestic economy built on conquest and slave labour, significant international trade with Europe, taxation systems, and an organised military. Dahomey was conquered in 1740 by the Oyo Empire, becoming her tributary state for a period before being subsequently defeated by the French in 1894 and annexed as part of a French colony in 1904. The Oyo Empire, on the other hand, was founded by the Yoruba people of modern-day Southwestern and North-Central Nigeria, as well as the southern and central Republic of Benin. The people are believed to have originated from the older Yoruba kingdom of Ile-Ife (or Ife), which already existed by the eight century. Archaeology has revealed that settlements in Ile-Ife showed features of urbanism in the twelfth to the fourteenth century. During the 1300s, the artists at Ile-Ife developed a refined and naturalistic sculptural tradition in terracotta, stone, copper, brass, and bronze, which, based on stylistic similarities with the Nok terracotta, are now believed to be a continuation of the traditions of the earlier Nokite culture. Ile-Ife remained the ancestral and spiritual homeland of the Yoruba people, while the Oyo Empire stood out as the dominant military and political power in Yorubaland. Oyo Empire emerged in the sixteenth century, suffered a temporary defeat by the Nupe Kingdom, and by the end of the sixteenth century, having overturned their defeat, expanded to a region spanning from the western region of the Niger to the hills of Togo, the Yoruba of Ketu, Dahomey, and the Fon nation. Due to her northern location, the empire served as middle-man in the north-south trade and in connecting the eastern forest of Guinea with western and central Sudan, the Sahara, and North Africa. The empire remained strong for about two hundred years before becoming a British protectorate in 1888 and finally ceased to exist in 1896 due to internal conflicts. Another historic empire in the region with close association with the Ile-Ife Kingdom is the Benin Empire. Tradition asserts that the Edo people became dissatisfied with the rule of a dynasty of semi-mythical kings, the Ogisos. In the thirteenth century, they invited Prince Oranmiyan of Ife, a legendary hunter, to rule them. His son Eweka is regarded as the first Oba (or king) of Benin, although authority would remain for many years with a hereditary order of local chiefs. Late in the thirteenth century, royal power began to assert itself under the Oba Ewedo and was firmly established under the most famous king, Ewuare the Great, described as a great warrior and magician. By the mid-fifteenth century, the empire was engaged in political expansion and consolidation under Ewuare. By the time of his death in c. 1480, the empire had extended to include Dahomey (in the west), the Niger Delta (in the east), along the west African coast, and to some parts of Yorubaland (in the north). By the mid-sixteenth century, the kingdom had extended from the Niger River delta in the east to what is now Lagos (once the capital of Nigeria) in the west. Instructively, Lagos was founded by a Benin army, and it continued to pay tribute to the Benin Empire until the end of the nineteenth century.

Contact between the empire and Europe was initiated in 1472 with the arrival of Portuguese explorer Ruy de Sequeira, culminating in trade relations between the Benin and Portuguese Empires. This contact with Europe was later to the contact with the Mediterranean as Benin had already related with the Mediterranean for at least 1,500 years before the contact with Europe during the fifteenth century. In an essay titled *100 Years after the Invasion of Benin Reflection*, Richard Akinjide, a former Attorney-General and Minister of Justice in Nigeria, states: "The Kingdom of Benin was already in continuous contact with nations of the Mediterranean for at least 1,500 years before the Europeans came to Benin. The kingdom's commercial and foreign relations were well established. It had its own money economy independent of the Europeans. The kingdom of Benin's own currency known as Ighos was accepted for trade and general means of exchange in East, West, and North Africa. The kingdom was part of the African Empires and Kingdoms independent and sovereign at a time when Europe was part of the Roman colonies."

By the early 1700s, Benin Empire was wrecked with dynastic disputes and internal conflicts. However, it regained much of its former power and glory shortly after during the reign of Oba Eresoyen, beginning from c. 1735. Oba Eresoyen is reported to have introduced the idea of banking in the empire. He also established the first bank in the empire by building a banking house known as Owigho or Aza. The empire was annexed by the British in 1897 during colonisation.

In the southeastern part of today's Nigeria existed the Kingdom of Nri, which the Igbo people of Nigeria founded. It rose in the tenth century as a religion-polity operated as a theocracy and was ruled by a priest-king known as Eze Nri (or King of Nri), whose religious and political influence extended to over a third of Igboland.

The kingdom is home to the Igbo-Ukwu culture, known for its highly sophisticated bronze metal-working, which employed bronze casting techniques using elephant-head motifs dating back to the ninth century. The bronzes of Igbo-Ukwu are comparable to those of Ile-Ife and Benin but are different, come from a different tradition, and existed centuries before the relatively more well-known Ile-Ife bronzes. Artefacts discovered from sites in Igbo-Ukwu territory include brass artefacts of local manufacture (some of which dated 850 AD and are now in the British Museum) and glass beads from Egypt or India, indicative of extra-regional trade.

The kingdom flourished well into the sixteenth century but appeared to have passed its peak in the eighteenth century, encroached upon and overshadowed by the rise of the Benin Kingdom and also the Igala Kingdom—which was founded by the Igala people who lived north of Igboland. Remnants of the kingdom persisted until the early twentieth century, when the area became part of the British colony in 1911.

SOUTHERN AFRICA

The Bantu people arrived in Southern Africa following the historic Bantu Expansion, and by the first millennium BC had well-established settlements in the region where they also initiated various civilisations. A pioneering group of Bantu migrants headed south to the upper Zambezi valley in the second century BC, resulting in new settlements which by the first century AD had extended to the savannahs of modern-day Malawi, Zambia, and Zimbabwe. The Kingdom of Mapungubwe was the first prominent kingdom in this region. It rose around the ninth century and was located at the confluence of the Shashe and Limpopo rivers. Its capital was at Mapungubwe (now a World Heritage Site). The kingdom lasted about eighty years and, at its height, had an estimated population of about five thousand people. Mapungubwean society is thought by archaeologists to be the first class-based social system in southern Africa, in that its leaders were separated from and were higher in rank than its other inhabitants. Although no written records have yet been found of life in the kingdom, archaeological excavations indicate a likelihood of a three-tiered hierarchy: With the commoners inhabiting low-lying sites, district leaders occupying small hilltops, and the capital at Mapungubwe hill serving as the supreme authority. The kingdom was ruled by a king—Thovhele Shiriyadenga Nemapungubwe—who divided the state into districts, each governed by his children as Paramount Chiefs, who reported directly to their father the king. After the collapse of Mapungubwe, the Kingdom of Zimbabwe arose in the region in c. 1220. The capital, Lusvingo (also Great Zimbabwe), had what is believed to be the largest stone structure in pre-colonial Southern Africa. The word "Zimbabwe" means "stone houses" in Shona. Great Zimbabwe was also a thriving trading centre from the eleventh to the fifteenth centuries. Sixteenth-century records left by Portuguese explorer and historian João de Barros suggest that Lusvingo might have been inhabited up to the early-1500s before it was later abandoned.

Although Portuguese explorers encountered her ruins in the sixteenth century, it was not until late in the nineteenth century that her existence was confirmed, consequently generating much archaeological research. Other European explorers who visited the site in the late-1800s believed it to be the legendary city of Ophir—the site of King Solomon's mines. Due to its sophisticated stonework and further evidence of advanced culture, the site was variously, but wrongly, attributed to ancient civilisations such as the Phoenician, Greek, or

Egyptian. Its medieval and exclusively African origin was later
confirmed in 1905 by the English archaeologist David
Randall-MacIver, whose findings received further confirmation
in 1929 by the English archaeologist Gertrude Caton-Thomp-
son.

At its peak, the Kingdom of Zimbabwe had over one
hundred and fifty tributary-states throughout the region under
its political influence, exercising political authority over a wider
area than her predecessor Mapungubwe. Upon her decline, the
Kingdom of Zimbabwe was succeeded by two smaller kingdoms:
Mutapa (in the north) and Butua (in the south), most of whose
territories were later absorbed by the Rozwi Empire which rose
late in the seventeenth century. The Rozwi Empire (also Rozvi)
was a Karanga empire founded in c. 1684 by Changamire Dombo,
who successfully fought off a Portuguese invasion aimed at taking
control of the gold trade in the region, and who went on to
establish an empire that dominated the plateau of modern-day
Zimbabwe. The Rozvi chiefs revived the tradition of building in
stone and constructed impressive cities, known as zimbabwes
(stone houses), throughout the region under Rozvi influence.
Polychrome pottery was also emblematic of Rozvi culture,
although agriculture formed the backbone of her economy. The
empire engaged in local and foreign trade importing goods such
as gun, salt, beads, and seashells in exchange for ivory, copper,
and gold. Portuguese records show the empire had sophisticated
military strategies, including the "cow-horn formation" later
adopted by Shaka Zulu in the nineteenth century. The Rozvi
empire disintegrated early in the nineteenth century, and the
Kingdom of Mthwakazi emerged as a successor, founded in the
early nineteenth-century by the Ndebele people under King

Mzilikazi. It had its capital at Bulawayo and a domain known as "Matabeleland" by the Europeans, which consisted of former Rozvi and other satellite territories. At its peak, the kingdom's domain encompassed the Limpopo and Zambezi areas to the north and south, the desert of the Makgadikgadi salt pans (or Botswana salt flats) to the west, and the realm of Gaza Empire (south of today's Mozambique) to the east. The discovery of gold in 1867, in Mashonaland (north of today's Zimbabwe), which was under the kingdom's sovereignty, resulted in an increased European interest in the affairs of the kingdom subsequently culminating in the death of King Mzilikazi in 1868. He was succeeded by his son, King Lobengula, who granted several concessions to the British, the most notable of them being the 1888 Rudd Concession which gave Cecil Rhodes exclusive mineral rights in much of the lands east of the kingdom's main territory. The Rudd Concession also permitted British mining and colonisation of Matabele lands between the Limpopo and Zambezi rivers. The kingdom ceased to exist in 1894 following British conquest and colonisation. The Bantu Nguni-speaking people founded the Ndwandwe Kingdom, in today's Zululand, late in the eighteenth century. Ndwandwe had a fractious relationship with the neighbouring Mthethwa kingdom in Zululand, with whom they fought several wars. In one of such wars, in 1817, the Ndwandwe under King Zwide destroyed Mthethwa kingdom under King Dingiswayo, resulting in the emergence of the legendary Shaka Zulu, who mobilised the remnant of Mthethwa against Ndwandwe. Shaka led the Zulus (also a Nguni people) against another invasion by Zwide in 1819, which resulted in the defeat of the latter culminating in the

disintegration of Ndwandwe. Several smaller splinter empires
emerged from the crumbled Ndwandwe kingdom, notable among
which was the aforementioned Gaza Empire. The Mthethwa
Empire was founded by the Nguni people in the eighteenth
century, as was her neighbouring empire Ndwandwe. The empire
functioned as a confederacy and was consolidated and extended
under the rule of Chief Dingiswayo. He allied with the Tsonga
people to the north, early in the nineteenth century, and began
trading with the Portuguese in today's Mozambique. In about
1811, the Buthelezi and a number of other Nguni clans were
integrated as part of the Mthethwa confederacy. Mthethwa was
superseded by the Zulu Kingdom led by Shaka, a former
lieutenant in the Mthethwa army. He later became King Shaka
Zulu following the death of Dingiswayo in the 1817 battle
between Mthethwa and Ndwandwe. The Zulu Kingdom stretched
along the Indian Ocean coast from the Tugela River in the south
to the Pongola River in the north. It grew to dominate much of
today's KwaZulu–Natal in South Africa. Under Shaka, a system
of fortified settlements known as "amakhanda" was established,
and young men were drafted into "amabutho" (regiments based
on age sets). Shaka was assassinated in 1828 and succeeded by his
half-brother Dingane, during whose reign the kingdom was
penetrated by the British, as well as the Boers, who had formed
an alliance with his brother Mpande. Dingane was deposed by
Mpande in 1840 and later killed, while in subsequent years, both
the Boers and the British usurped portions of the Zulu territory.
In 1879 during the reign of Cetshwayo (Mpande's son), the
British invaded the kingdom resulting in the Anglo-Zulu War,
which culminated in the demise of the kingdom and its eventual

absorption in 1910 into the Colony of Natal as part of the Union of South Africa.

The foregoing historical summary represents a small fraction of Africa's history, which is relatively hidden. A greater part of Africa's rich history is relatively untold, particularly her history before her colonisation by Europe from late in the nineteenth century; hence they have remained hidden for centuries. On the contrary, the popular history of Africa is the one authored by European historians whose stories are characterised by bias, pervasive prejudice, inaccuracies, incompleteness, and distortion. It probably would not be too far from the truth, suggesting that the story of Africa as told by European writers constituted mainly of propaganda which is primarily aimed at misinforming instead of informing.

The need to misinform is perhaps necessary in order to deny Africa and the African people knowledge of their true identity and heritage, without which they would remain vulnerable and susceptible to control and manipulation. Rediscovering their true identity and heritage is imperative if Africa and the African people would stand any chance of liberating themselves from foreign control and manipulation, including those perpetrated internally through her leadership.

An important revelation from the true history of Africa is that Africa was great in times past—it is the place where civilisation was birthed. Africa originated trade and commerce, science and technology, the system of formal education, military methods and equipment, and was very independent of the rest of the world for several millennia until her colonisation from late in the nineteenth century. It is instructive to note that although historic slavery dealt a very hard blow to Africa, it was her subsequent colonisation that brought her down to her knees while ensuring she eventually became flat-faced on the ground. Sadly, Africa continues to lie prostrate on the ground, unable to stir or rouse herself, having become laden with various burdens imposed on her through different measures and strategies adopted for her perpetual domination through neocolonialism. As revealed in the foregoing historical narrative, Africa's indigenous kingdoms and states were all forcefully brought to an end during colonisation. Any few kingdoms or states which survived during colonisation became reduced to mere ceremonial kingdoms with little or no political power. In order to ensure permanence to the end of these ancient African kingdoms, empires, and states, countries, nation-states, provinces, or protectorates were constituted by the colonial powers for ease of control and administration, geared towards exploitation and manipulation. Incidentally, this colonial construct remains the defining criterion for the overall classification and administration of Africa and the African people till date.

This remains, in my opinion, the single most difficult challenge for Africa, constituting a huge obstacle on the path of freedom and progress for the African people, for the simple reason that a house divided is bound to crumble into a great fall. These divisions invented under colonisation continue to stand in the way of unity between different neighbouring African peoples. Therefore, Africa and her people must look beyond these imaginary boundaries in order to foster the degree of unity required to win back full control of local resources, thus securing true independence at last.

Outside Africa also, there are other aspects of hidden history directly related to Africa, represented in civilisations in other parts of the world which were birthed, shaped, or heavily influenced by Africa and the African people. We shall explore very few of such civilisations with a highly summarised outline.

OTHER CIVILISATIONS INFLUENCED BY AFRICA

The Mediterranean region holds a very interesting history of famous ancient civilisations such as the Babylonian Empire and the ancient Greek and Roman Empires. It has been noted that a significant part of the Mediterranean coasts is part of the tectonic plate of Africa, but which today is referred to as the Middle East. It was also noted that this development was mainly for political rather than geographical reasons. Based on geography alone, places such as today's Jordan, Israel, Syria, Saudi Arabia, Iraq, Iran, and parts of Turkey would rightly be defined as an extension of Northeastern Africa. Consequently, historic ancient civilisations that existed in the specified region would rightly be considered African or at least heavily influenced by African cultures and peoples. It has also been noted that the early humans first existed in Africa before spreading across the world and that sometime after the Great Flood, which saw to the destruction of the Old World, the descendants of the only survivors—Noah and his family—had reached "the land of Shinar" where the plan to construct the Towel of Babel was conceived and initiated

(Genesis 11:2). The historic Nimrod, who descended from Noah through Ham and Cush, is traditionally associated with this rebellion and is thought to be the leader of the people associated with constructing the tower at Babel. In the Book of Genesis, he was described as "a mighty one in the earth" and was reported to have established a kingdom in the land of Shinar situated in the southern region of Mesopotamia. During the time of Nimrod, humanity consisted entirely of closely-knit communities descended from a single-family, with the significant deduction that the kingdom associated with Nimrod and any other contemporary kingdoms during this historical period would rightly be described as African (and "black" too). This assumption is corroborated by the writings of the first-century Jewish historian Flavius Josephus.

In his 20-volume historical work, *Antiquities of the Jews*, Josephus writes in the second paragraph of the sixth chapter of Vol. 1: "The children of Ham possessed the land from Syria and Amanus [Nur Mountains in Turkey] and the mountains of Libanus [Lebanon], seizing upon all that was on its sea coasts; and as far as the ocean; and keeping it as their own. Some indeed of its names are utterly vanished away; others of them being changed, and another sound given them, are hardly to be discovered: yet a few there are which have kept their denominations intire [entire]. For of the four sons of Ham, time has not at all hurt the name of Chus [Cush]; for the Ethiopians, over whom he reigned, are even at this day, both by themselves, and by all men in Asia, called Chusites [Cushites]." This description reveals the expanse and extent of the boundaries of Cush; a term, like Ethiopia, which has been used to refer to Africa in different past times. This is very important because it implies that successive historical kingdoms in this region of the Mediterranean had African origin or at least were heavily influenced by Africa and Africans. This would have been the case until in later historic periods, following the emergence of the lighter skin tone in northern Asia, when light-skinned Asians began to arrive in the Mediterranean.

Phoenicia is a very popular historic ancient civilisation in the Mediterranean closely associated with Africa although thought to be of Semitic origin. Phoenicians who had interactions with other groups in Northern Africa in prehistoric periods established the Carthaginian empire, centred in Tunisia, in 814 BC. Although their actual origin seems to be shrouded in secrecy because no records about them, by them survived, they are thought to have arrived in the Mediterranean around 3000 BC. The name "Phoenicia" was given to them by Greek historians and inspired by the unique purple dye they produced. Phoenicia came from the Greek *phoinos*, meaning "blood red" or purple. It is, however, believed the people referred to themselves as Kena'ani (Canaani, or Canaanites), which somehow associates them with Canaan—a son of Ham and brother to Cush. Could the Phoenicians originally have come from Canaan? The names Canaan and Canaanite occur in cuneiforms, Egyptian and Phoenician writings from about the fifteenth century BC, and the Hebrew Bible or Old Testament Bible. Based on these sources, the location given for Canaan includes the whole of today's Palestine and Syria, the land west of the Jordan River, and, a strip of coastal land from Acre (or Akko, in Northwest Israel) northward. Interestingly, these locations all fall under the land of Cush, as described by Josephus in his historiography.

The earliest Greek civilisation in the Mediterranean—Minoan—also had a strong African influence. Minoan flourished between 3000 and 1100 BC and was centred at the Island of Crete—the first high civilisation in Greece. Although believed to have mysteriously disappeared, evidence of the possible presence of an ancient civilisation at Crete was first discovered by Archaeologist Arthur Evans, early in the twentieth century, as a result of surviving carved seal stones worn by native Cretans. This discovery led to excavation at Knossos, an ancient Cretan palace, from 1900 to 1905. The extensive ruins discovered confirmed the existence of the Minoan as an ancient Greek civilisation.

Although there is a lack of consensus among modern scholars on the ethnic origin of the Minoan civilisation, archaeological and anecdotal evidence point to Africa and black culture. Greek historians of the Classical Period attest that the foremost civilisations in ancient Greece—Minoan and Mycenaean—were founded by "foreigners" whom they referred to as "Pelasgians" (a collective term for all pre-Classical inhabitants of Greece), who arrived the Aegean from Africa in successive waves. A Malinke-speaking (or Mandinka) people originally from the Fezzan area (in today's Libya), known as Garamantes (also Carians), are believed to have arrived first. These earlier settlers described in classical Latin literature as "black" or "dark-skinned"—for example, *perusti* (Lucan 4.679) and *nigri* (Anthologia Latina 155 no.183)—are believed to have founded Crete, Thrace, and Attica, based on archaeology. Archaeology also revealed strong ancient Egyptian influences in the early art of the Minoans as well as in their later export trade, notably the exchange of pottery, oil, and wine in return for precious objects like copper and ivory. Minoan arts, notably pottery and paintings, also exhibit close similarity to those present in ancient Egypt. Furthermore, Greek epics such as the Aeneid, Illiad, and Odyssey, inspired by Minoan legends, show their stories to be about African people upon closer scrutiny. For instance, the long shields used by the heroes of these tales are similar to those used in Africa in contrast to the rounded ones more common in Eurasia. Perhaps adding to the uncertainty about its origin is the fact that the Minoan civilisation existed in several stages over several millennia, with successive migratory waves from different regions contributing to archaeological remains in the area where the civilisation existed.

The Minoan civilisation was succeeded by the Mycenaean civilisation which developed in mainland Greece in the second millennium BC, from the fifteenth to the thirteenth century BC. Historical records indicate that the Minoan civilisation significantly influenced the Mycenaean civilisation at the earlier stages: Pelasgians arriving in successive migratory waves from Northern and Eastern Africa, and the Levant in the Mediterranean founded major Mycenaean cities of Thebes and Athens, according to ancient Greek sources—Athens (Plutarch in Theses 12, and Ovid in Metamorphosis VII 402), and Thebes (Herodotus VII 91). A recent genetic study of the DNA sequence of the Bronze Age inhabitants of mainland Greece, Crete, and southwestern Anatolia by an international team of researchers from the University of Washington, the Harvard Medical School, and the Max Planck Institute for the Science of Human History, together with archaeologists and other collaborators in Greece and Turkey, which was reported in Nature on August 2, 2017, showed Minoans and

Mycenaeans were genetically highly similar but not identical, and also that some modern Greeks descended from these ancient populations. Significantly, the study also revealed that although both Minoans and Mycenaeans had some shared genetic origins, Mycenaeans had an additional minor genetic component absent in Minoans, which was traced to northern Eurasia.

This finding confirms both Minoan and Mycenaean civilisations to have been influenced by different successive migratory waves. The origin of Minoan, however, is undoubtedly African based on historiography and limited archaeology. Scholars have noted that "so much which characterise Minoan Crete seem wholly alien to latter Greece" thus confirming the founding population in Minoan to be different from the people who lived in Greece in later periods.

Similarly, the ancient Roman civilisation, which succeeded ancient Greek civilisations in exercising dominant control in that region of the Mediterranean, also had a significant African influence. In Roman historiography, ancient Rome refers to the civilisation which originated with the founding of the ancient city of Rome in the eighth century BC, lasting till the fifth century AD. Rome was different from Greek city-states, which excluded foreigners and subjected peoples to political participation because it incorporated conquered peoples into its social and political system. Allies and subjects who adopted Roman ways were eventually permitted citizenship. It was notable for its military prowess, and some of her rulers were army generals who came to power through conquest. One of Rome's former rulers was Emperor Lucius Septimius Severus Pertinax (or simply Septimius Severus). He was born in c. 145 or 146 AD in Leptis Magna, Tripolitania (an ancient city in today's Libya), to a Libyan father and a mother of Roman descent. Septimius was Roman emperor from 193–211 AD. His father Geta, was of Berber origin. Septimius was succeeded by his sons Geta and Caracalla.

Roman historiography also attests to the presence of significant black African populations in ancient Rome. At the height of the Roman Empire, most of Europe was under Roman dominion, resulting in African and black populations especially in Southern Europe, e.g., Britain, Portugal, and Spain. British author and journalist Peter Fryer gave a detailed account of black people in Roman Britain in his book *Staying Power: The History of Black People in Britain* (University of Alberta, 1984). He writes: "There were Africans in Britain before the English came here. They were soldiers in the Roman imperial army that occupied the southern part of our island for three and a half centuries. Among the troops defending Hadrian's wall in the third century AD was a "division of Moors" (numerus Maurorum Aurelianorum) named after Marcus Aurelius or a later emperor known officially by the same name." This Moorish unit, Peter went on to elaborate, was stationed at the Roman fortress of Aballava (now Burgh by Sands, near Carlisle), and was listed in an official register of the Roman administrative system known as a Notitia Dignitatum. The Moors established civilisation in parts of southern Europe and are reported to have ruled in Portugal. There is also an inscription referring to the unit on a third-century altar stone discovered in 1934 in the foundations of an old cottage in Beaumont during its demolition. The earliest attested date for the unit's presence in Britain is between 253–258 AD.

An important deduction here is that Africans, including Black Africans, already existed in Europe under Roman domination long before modern Europeans began their exploration during the fifteenth century, which brought them in contact with Africa and Africans.

In the Americas also, some ancient civilisations in the Mesoamerican region had African influence. For instance, the Olmec culture, which existed in Mesoamerica between 1200 and 400 BC, shows a close association with Africa. US-born historian Leo Wiener in his book *Africa and the Discovery of America* (Read Books, 2011), noted some similarities between Mandinka (West Africa) and native Mesoamerican (North America) religious symbols and words that have Mande roots and share similar meanings across both cultures. Also, the discovery of the now popular Olmec colossal heads at Tres Zapotes (in Mexico) in 1862 presents possible archaeological evidence connecting Mesoamerica with Africa. Apart from their massive size, seventeen confirmed Olmec heads from four Mesoamerican sites have distinguishing features, which include thick lips, big flat nose, large forehead, large earspools inserted into the ear lobes, and braided hair at the back of the head—features which are characteristic of black African people. This evidence has led scholars like José Maria Melgar y Serrano, who discovered the first head in 1862, to suggest an African origin for the Olmec. Other scholars in support of an African origin include Alfonso Medellin Zenil and Ivan van Sertima.

However, other scholars like Richard Diehl and Ann

Cyphers disagree, opting instead for an Asian origin but mainly because the possibility of pre-Columbian contact between Africa and the Americas has previously been questioned. But not anymore, as fresh evidence has recently come up attesting to a pre-Columbian contact—the voyage of Abu Bakr II to the Americas from western African about two hundred years before Columbus reached the Caribbean.

The recent unearthing of this previously unknown feat, contained in the oral history told by local historians known as griots, inspired the research by Malian scholar Gaoussou Diawara. Gaoussou's findings are in his book, *The Saga of Abubakari II*. Incidentally, the expedition by Abu Bakr II is somewhat corroborated by Christopher Columbus himself. According to the abstract of Columbus' log as recorded by an aid, Bartolomé de las Casas, the purpose of Columbus' third voyage was to confirm two claims: First was the claim of King John II of Portugal that "canoes had been found which set out from the coast of Guinea [West Africa] and sailed to the west with merchandise." The other was claims by some native inhabitants of the Caribbean Islands of Hispaniola that "from the south and the southeast had come black people whose spears were made of a metal called guanin." Chemical analyses of the gold tips on the spears found by Columbus in the Americas have confirmed them to be of possible West African origin. Both claims tend to confirm Abu Bakr's journey and pre-Columbian contact between Africa and the Americas, thereby eliminating any doubts about the African origin of the Olmec heads.

In addition to the Olmec heads, there are other forms of evidence, including those related to epigraphy. Scholars have noted a close similarity between ancient writing systems in

Mesoamerica and Africa. Mesoamerican writing systems, such as the Maya inscriptions, have been proposed by scholars like Constantine Samuel Rafinesque to be most likely related to Libyco-Berber writing of Africa. Furthermore, osteology presents yet some more evidence showing that at least some of the Olmec people were of African origin: Cranial evidence from two Mesoamerican sites; Tlatilco and Cerro de las Mesas (in Mexico), show that 14% and 4.5% of the skeletal remains from both sites respectively had "elements of Black racial composition," according to a study by Anthropologist Andrzej Wierciñski.

It is instructive to note that the Olmec greatly influenced the two major historic civilisations in the Americas—Aztec and Mayan.

Thus was the extent of Africa's influence in some of the world's most historic civilisations within and outside Africa, e.g., Egyptian, Greek, Roman, Phoenician, Aztec, and Mayan. Sadly, this part of Africa's history is relatively hidden, having been excluded from the popular historical narratives which form part of the history taught under formal education. Thanks to credible and objective scholarship, coupled with various advancements in science and technology, some of Africa's previously hidden history is gradually being unearthed, although most of these fresh narratives are yet to become popular because they are yet to make it to the academic curricula of the mainstream global educational system, except in some specialised disciplines offered in some universities.

African countries could blaze the trail in this regard by including these hidden histories of Africa in their academic curricula at all levels of formal education, rather than wait upon the global West to do the inclusion.

CHAPTER FOUR

Hebrew

Civilisations

The Hebrews are another ancient dark-skinned or black people with an origin in the Mediterranean region. It has been noted that the earliest people in the Mediterranean were originally black, before the later arrival of migrants of Asian descent to the region subsequently resulted in the prominence of the lighter skin variant as a result of interbreeding. Hebrew refers to the descendants of the biblical patriarch Abraham (Hebrew *Avraham*), originally called Abram (Hebrew *Avram*).

The origin of the term Hebrew itself is uncertain. However, it could be derived from the word *eber*, or *ever*, which in Hebrew means the "other side," a possible reference to

Abraham's crossing into the land of Canaan from the "other side" of the Euphrates or Jordan River. The term Hebrew almost always occurs in the Hebrew Bible (or the Old Testament Bible) as a name given to the Israelites by other people, as opposed to one used by themselves. The Israelites are descendants of Abraham through Isaac and Jacob (also called Israel, Genesis 33:28). The name Hebrew could also be related to the seminomadic Habiru people recorded in Egyptian inscriptions of the thirteenth and twelfth BC as having settled in Egypt.

Biblical scholars use the term Hebrews to designate the descendants of Abraham through Isaac and Jacob, particularly from the time the patriarch crossed over into the land of Canaan until their conquest of Canaan late in the second millennium BC. However, the term could rightly be applied to every descendant of Abraham because it was his crossing over into the land of Canaan that gave cause to the term in the first place. Abraham, who would become the father of many nations, flourished early in the second millennium BC and was the first of the Hebrew patriarchs.

The Book of Genesis presents a partial biography of Abraham, which traces his ancestry all the way back to Shem, Noah's son. The following lineage is provided for Abraham in Genesis 11: 10–32: *These are the records of the generations of Shem [from whom Abraham descended]. Shem was a hundred years old when he became the father of Arpachshad, two years after the flood. And Shem lived five hundred years after Arpachshad was born, and he had other sons and daughters. When Arpachshad had lived thirty-five years, he became the father of Shelah. Arpachshad lived four hundred and three years after Shelah was born, and he had other sons and daughters. When Shelah had lived thirty years, he became the father of Eber. Shelah lived four hundred and three years after Eber was born, and he had other sons and daughters. When Eber had lived thirty-four years, he became the father of Peleg. And Eber lived four hundred and thirty years after Peleg was born, and he had other sons and daughters. When Peleg had lived thirty years, he became the father of Reu. And Peleg lived two hundred and nine years after Reu was born, and he had other sons and daughters. When Reu had lived thirty-two years, he became the father of Serug. And Reu lived two hundred and seven years after Serug was born, and he had other sons and daughters. When Serug had lived thirty years, he became the father of Nahor. And Serug lived two hundred years after Nahor was born, and he had other sons and daughters. When Nahor had lived twenty-nine years, he became the father of Terah. And Nahor lived a hundred and nineteen years after Terah was born, and he had other sons and daughters. After Terah had lived seventy years, he became the father of Abram and Nahor and Haran [his firstborn]. Now these are the records of the descendants of Terah. Terah was the father of Abram (Abraham), Nahor, and Haran; and Haran was the father of Lot. Haran died before his father Terah in the land of his birth, in Ur of the Chaldeans. Abram and Nahor took wives for themselves. The name of Abram's wife was Sarai (later called Sarah), and the name of Nahor's wife was Milcah, the daughter of Haran, the father of Milcah and Iscah. But Sarai was barren; she did not have a child. Terah took Abram his son, and Lot the son of Haran, his grandson, and Sarai his daughter-in-law, his son Abram's wife; and they went out together to go from Ur of the*

Chaldeans into the land of Canaan; but when they came to Haran [about five hundred and fifty miles northwest of Ur], they settled there. Terah lived two hundred and five years; and Terah died in Haran (AMP).

Based on biblical account, Abraham's origin is in the Ur of the Chaldeans (Ur Kasdim), and of the clan of Terah. Also, tradition is particularly firm on this point. Most scholars agree Ur Kasdim is the Sumerian city of Ur, today's Tall al-Muqayyar (or Mughair), about two hundred miles southeast of Baghdad in lower Mesopotamia, which was excavated from 1922 to 1934. Kasdim is the same as the Kaldu of the cuneiform texts at Mari. Abraham subsequently left Ur, in Mesopotamia, in obedience to God's call and promise recorded thus: *Now the Lord had said unto Abram, Get thee out of thy country, and from thy kindred, and from thy father's house, unto a land that I will show thee: and I will make of thee a great nation, and I will bless thee, and make thy name great; and thou shalt be a blessing: and I will bless them that bless thee, and curse him that curseth thee: and in thee shall all families of the earth be blessed* (Genesis 12: 1–3 KJV).

Abraham, upon departing from Ur, eventually arrived in the land of Canaan (somewhere between today's Syria and Egypt). Abraham's firstborn son was Ishmael, who was born of Hagar (Sarah's maid), but Isaac, who was later conceived by his wife Sarah, became the fulfilment of the promise God made to Abraham (see Genesis 15; 17: 19–20).

Ishmael settled in the Desert of Paran and had twelve sons with his Egyptian wife: Neba'joth, Kedar, Ad'beel, Mibsam, Mishma, Dumah, Massa, Hadar, Tema, Jetur, Naphish, and Ked'emah. Ishmael's twelve sons stretched across the region from Havilah to Shur (from Assyria to the borders of Egypt).

Traditionally, the Ishmaelites are associated with Arabs (specifically, North Arabians). Note that the original Arabs were very dark-skinned compared to most of their modern-day counterparts.

Indeed, two prominent historic North Arabian kingdoms: the Qedarite Kingdom and the Nabataean Kingdom, have names very similar to two of Ishmael's sons. Assyrian and Babylonian royal inscriptions and North Arabian inscriptions from ninth to sixth century BC mention the king of Qedar, while the names Nabat, Kedar, Abdeel, Dumah, Massa, and Teman—names of Ishmael's sons—were mentioned in the Assyrian royal inscriptions as Arabian tribes. The Qedarite Kingdom continued long after the demise of the last native Babylonian king, Nabonidus. However, the Nabataean Kingdom emerged from the Qedarite Kingdom, as evidenced by geography and language continuity between the two kingdoms some two hundred and fifty years later.

Isaac, the child of promise, had himself a set of twins—Esau and Jacob. Esau took wives from the Canaanites and also from the house of his uncle Ishmael. Allying with the Ishmaelites, he was able to drive the Horites out of Mount Seir (in Canaan) to settle in that region. Genesis 36 gives a comprehensive list of Esau's descendants, referring to him as "the father of the Edomites in mount Seir." The ancient kingdom of Edom (also Edam or Adum) was located between Moab to the northeast, the Arabah to the west, and the Arabian desert to the south and east, and appears in Egyptian and Mesopotamian records. Amalek was another prominent kingdom that descended from Esau. After the birth of Esau and Jacob, following the demise of Sarah, Abraham married Keturah with whom he had six more sons: Zimran, Jokshan, Medan, Mid'i-an, Ishbak, and Shu'ah.

All of the aforementioned kingdoms or civilisations and several others founded by the descendants of Abraham through Ishmael and Esau, and also by the sons of Keturah and their descendants, rightly qualify to be referred to as Hebrew civilisations also, and belong in the overall Hebrew family since they all descended from Abraham, the first Hebrew.

Jacob, Esau's twin brother, was the child through whom God's promise to Abraham would be accomplished. The descendants of Jacob—Israelites—constitute the primary subject of this book and so would be treated more extensively.

Israelites

Historically, Israelites are the descendants of Jacob's twelve sons (Israel): Reuben, Simeon, Levi, Judah, Dan, Naphtali, Gad, Asher, Issachar, Zebulun, Joseph, and Benjamin. The nation of Israel was formed while in captivity in Egypt. Her people emerged several centuries later to establish an independent nationhood in the land promised to Abraham by God—the land of Canaan. The exact extent of the land promised Israel is noted in different passages in the Hebrew Bible, including the following: *I will establish your borders from the **Red Sea** to the **Sea of the Philistines** (the Mediterranean), and from the wilderness to the **River Euphrates**; for I will hand over the residents of the land to you, and you shall drive them out before you* (Exodus 23:31 AMP). Also this: *On the same day the LORD made a covenant* *(promise, pledge) with Abram, saying, "To your descendants I have given this land, From the **river of Egypt** to the great **river Euphrates**— [the land of] the Kenites and the Kenizzites and the Kadmonites and the Hittites and the Perizzites and the Rephaim, the Amorites and the Canaanites and the Girgashites and the Jebusites"* (Genesis 15: 18–21 AMP). And this: *Then the LORD spoke to Moses, saying, "Command the Israelites, 'When you enter the land of Canaan, this is the land that shall be yours as an inheritance, the land of Canaan according to its boundaries, your southern region shall be from the Wilderness of Zin along the side of Edom, and your southern boundary from the end of the Salt (Dead) Sea eastward. Your boundary shall turn from the south to the ascent of Akrabbim, and continue on to Zin, and its limit shall be south of Kadesh-barnea. Then it shall go on to Hazar-addar and pass on to Azmon. Then the boundary shall turn from Azmon to the Brook of Egypt (Wadi el-arish), and its limit shall be at the [Mediterranean] Sea. 'As the western boundary you shall have the Great [Mediterranean] Sea and its coastline. This shall be your western boundary. 'And this shall be your north border: from the Great [Mediterranean] Sea mark out your boundary line to Mount Hor; from Mount Hor you shall mark out your boundary to the entrance of Hamath, and the limit of the border shall be at Zedad; then the [northern] boundary shall go on to Ziphron, and its limit shall be at Hazar-enan. This shall be your northern boundary. 'You shall mark out your eastern boundary from Hazar-enan to Shepham; the [eastern] boundary shall go down from Shepham to Riblah on the east side of Ain and shall descend and reach to the slope on the east of the Sea of Chinnereth [the Sea of Galilee]; and the [eastern] boundary shall go down to the Jordan [River], and its limit shall be at the Salt*

(Dead) Sea. This shall be your land according to its boundaries all around'" So Moses commanded the Israelites, saying, "This is the land you are to inherit by lot, which the LORD has commanded to be given to the nine tribes and the half-tribe [of Manasseh] (Numbers 34: 1–13 AMP).

The Red Sea and the Euphrates are mentioned to define the southern and eastern borders of the full land promised the Israelites. It is important to point out that the Red Sea corresponding to the Hebrew *Yam Suf* was understood in ancient times to be the Erythraean Sea, as reflected in the Septuagint translation. Although the English name "Red Sea" is derived from the name "Erythraean," which in turn is derived from the Greek for red, the term denotes all the waters surrounding Arabia, including the Indian Ocean and the Persian Gulf, and not merely the sea lying to the west of Arabia bearing this name in modern English. Thus, the entire Arabian Peninsula lies within the borders described. Although modern maps depicting the region take a reticent view, often leaving the southern and eastern borders vaguely defined, the borders of the land given in the Book of Numbers have a precisely defined eastern border, including the Arabah and Jordan. Note that the land was divided among the sons of Israel as previously listed except that instead of Joseph, his two sons, Ephraim and Manasseh, were allocated portions while the tribe of Levi had no allocation but instead were scattered across the other tribes to serve as priests.

The aforementioned boundaries represent the land promised to Israel, which the people were meant to take over through military conquest. The actual territory settled by the

Israelites is commonly described in the Hebrew Bible as "from Dan to Beersheba," as the Israelites never really conquered the entire land promised to them before they were subsequently conquered and scattered from the region.

Events leading to the actual formation of Israel as a nation first started with the migration of Jacob and his immediate family into Egypt to escape a famine in the region which also affected Canaan (Genesis 41: 54; 46: 1–34). By this time, Joseph, the eleventh son of Jacob, was already in Egypt and had become next in command to Pharaoh after experiencing a series of personal vicissitudes, which included enslavement and wrongful imprisonment. Pharaoh instructed Joseph to tell his brothers, who had come to buy grain in Egypt, to return to Canaan and bring the entire family over to Egypt to be resettled (Genesis 41: 38–44; 46: 17–19).

This mass migration of the children of Israel into Egypt had earlier been revealed to Abraham by God thus: *God said to Abram, "Know for sure that your descendants will be strangers [living temporarily] in a land (Egypt) that is not theirs, where they will be enslaved and oppressed for four hundred years.* (Genesis 15:13 AMP). The children of Israel lived freely and prospered in Egypt for many years until: a new king arose over Egypt, who did not know Joseph [nor the history of his accomplishments] (Exodus 1: 8 AMP). This pharaoh's identity is uncertain, but some scholars think he was Ahmose I (1570–1546 BC), founder of the eighteenth dynasty of Egypt's New Kingdom, or Ahmose's successor, Amenhotep I (1546–1525 BC). Others believe he was one of the first of the Hyksos rulers. Thenceforth, Israel's fortunes in Egypt changed drastically, culminating in enslavement and mistreatment. Exodus 1–14 detail this period in Israel's history up to their eventual departure from Egypt and their miraculous crossing of the Red Sea into the wilderness. They travelled for several years until eventually arriving in Canaan. Israel departed from Egypt in the thirteenth century BC, under the leadership of Moses, and are believed to have entered Canaan in c. 1250 BC, settling at first in the hill country and the south. They had a checkered history in the land promised to them as they were severally conquered and expelled from the land at different periods due to breaching the covenant God made with their father Abraham—the Abrahamic Covenant.

Much of what scholars know about Israel's ancient history comes from the Hebrew Bible, which contains a wealth of information relating to their origin and history. The key aspect of Israel's history most relevant to this discourse relates to the expulsion of the true Israelites from their land and is hereby summarised.

DIVIDED AND CONQUERED

The first king of Israel was King Saul but Kings David and Solomon are the more historically popular past rulers of Israel. King David ruled Israel in c. 1000 BC while his son King Solomon who succeeded him, is credited with building the historic First Temple in ancient Jerusalem. After King Solomon's death, the Kingdom of Israel was divided into two kingdoms in c. 931 BC, under the reign of his son King Rehoboam: Kingdom of Israel (also called Samaria or Ephraim) in the north and Kingdom of Judah in the south. While Rehoboam ruled over the southern kingdom, Jeroboam ruled over the northern kingdom as her first king. King Jeroboam, once a servant of King Solomon, was of the tribe of Ephraim.

A people divided become vulnerable and easy to conquer. This proved true in the case of Israel because shortly after the kingdom became divided into two, both factions eventually fell. The northern kingdom was the first to be conquered through a gradual process spanning several years; the Assyrian conquest of the northern kingdom started in c. 740 BC under King Pul and is recorded in Israel's chronicles thus: *So the God of Israel stirred up the spirit of Pul, king of Assyria, [that is,] the spirit of Tilgath-pilneser king of Assyria, and he carried them away into exile—the Reubenites, the Gadites, and the half-tribe of Manasseh—and brought them to Halah, Habor, Hara, and the river Gozan, [where they remain] to this day* (1 Chronicles 5: 26 AMP). It is important to note the first batch of Israelites expelled from their land and the immediate locations they were taken to—places in Assyria, in northern Mesopotamia. Some from this group of Israelites or their descendants could have subsequently ventured outside Assyria further into other neighbouring places where they could have been assimilated into such populations and cultures. Very importantly, none of the people expelled from the northern kingdom of Israel or their descendants ever returned to their original land in ancient Israel from whence they or their ancestors were expelled, "to this day."

In c. 722 BC, the capital city of the northern kingdom, Samaria, was conquered by the Assyrians under Shalmaneser V after a siege that began three years earlier. This event is recorded in the Hebrew Bible thus: *Then the king of Assyria invaded all the land [of Israel] and went up to Samaria and besieged it for three years. In the ninth year of Hoshea, the king of Assyria took*

*Samaria and carried [the people of] Israel into exile to Assyria,
and settled them in Halah and in Habor, by the river of Gozan,
and in the cities of the Medes.* (2 Kings 17: 5–6 AMP). Thus the
northern kingdom of Israel was completely sacked and overtaken
by Assyrians while her people would remain in exile to this day,
having been possibly assimilated into other cultures and
populations. The northern kingdom of Israel never existed again
in any form, either with full or partial autonomy.

A few centuries later, it was the turn of the southern
kingdom, Judah, to be conquered. The Babylonians under
Nebuchadnezzar II began a siege of Jerusalem late in 589 BC,
culminating in the destruction of the city and the First Temple
in 586 BC. A Second Temple replaced the first in c. 516 BC. This
bit of Judah's history is recorded in the Hebrew Bible thus: *Then
Nebuzaradan the captain of the bodyguard deported [into exile]
the rest of the people who were left in the city and the deserters
who had joined the king of Babylon, and the rest of the multitude.
But the captain of the bodyguard left some of the unimportant
and poorest people of the land to be vineyard workers and farmers*
(2 Kings 25: 11–12 AMP). Here, the people of the southern
kingdom are shown to have been expelled to Babylon, where,
again, most would subsequently be assimilated.

Following the fall of Babylon to the Achaemenid Empire
(also called the First Persian Empire) under Cyrus the Great in
539 BC, some Judean exiles returned to Jerusalem, inaugurating
the formative period in the development of a distinctive Judahite
identity in the province of Yehud Medinata—Province of Judah.
Following her initial conquest by the Babylonians, Judah never
again regained full autonomy as an independent kingdom;

instead, it maintained an existence as an administrative province, first of the Babylonian Empire and subsequently, Achaemenid Empire. The Books of Ezra and Nehemiah detail the return of Israelite exiles to Jerusalem and Judah from Babylon and the rebuilding of the temple.

A very interesting historical piece is that it was following this return to Jerusalem that the people of Israel would come to be referred to by writers as "Jews." However, it is imperative to clarify that only a token population of Israelites returned to Judah during this mass return and not the entire population of Israel. The whole population of the northern kingdom or their descendants never returned to their land to this day. Therefore, if the term "Jew" refers to someone from the Kingdom of Judah, then "Jews" could not rightly be used to represent the people of Israel collectively. Just as "New Yorker" or "Londoner" could not rightly be used to represent the entire people of the US or England, respectively. It is also noted here, for future reference, that the term "Jew" is also used to refer to any person whose religion is Judaism.

This latter application is the more common use of the term, especially starting from the nineteenth century. This latter definition and application of the word Jew—as a practitioner of Judaism—is particularly relevant in relation to the present nation of Israel and her citizens. Today's Israel is simply a Jewish state or, putting it differently, a nation composed mainly and exclusively of practitioners of Judaism. It became constituted as a nation in 1948 when David Ben-Gurion, who became the first prime minister, proclaimed the creation of the State of Israel around 4 pm on May 14, 1948—the day the British mandate over

Palestine was formally terminated. The events which culminated in the declaration of a State of Israel started with successive migrations of practitioners of Judaism—Jews—in small numbers into the Palestine region, mainly due to persecution. It is noted here that a majority of these Jews were of European descent.

The birth of modern Zionism late in the nineteenth century encouraged more Jewish migration into the Palestine region, particularly from eastern Europe, where there was a growing level of persecution of practitioners of Judaism. Between 1882 and 1903, an estimated thirty-five thousand Jews migrated to the region during the First Aliyah. The Jewish population in the region continued to rise such that by 1890, Jews constituted a majority in Jerusalem. Another forty thousand Jews migrated to the region between 1904 and 1914 during the Second Aliyah. In 1908, the Zionist organisation set up the 'Eretz Israel Office' in Jaffa and began to adopt a systematic Jewish settlement policy, and in 1909, residents of Jaffa established the first entirely Yiddish-speaking city, Ahuzat Bayit, later renamed Tel Aviv.

The British assumed control of the Palestine region after World War I, following the defeat of the Ottoman Empire, subsequently issuing the Balfour Declaration in November 1917 announcing its intention to facilitate the "establishment in Palestine of a national home for the Jewish people." The Balfour Declaration was later endorsed by the League of Nations (the predecessor of the United Nations) in 1922 to facilitate Jewish immigration and settlement in the region. A move that resulted in the Arabs in the region stepping up their attacks on the Jewish migrants. Jewish settlement in the region was significantly increased after World War II ended, as many Jewish survivors of the Holocaust were encouraged to immigrate there.

The British subsequently relinquished their control of Palestine to the United Nations, who, on November 19, 1947, recommended the partitioning of Palestine into two states: Jewish and Arab. As previously noted, the termination of the British mandate over Palestine inspired the declaration of the State of Israel by Ben-Gurion. Thus, today's Israel and her people are primarily Jews (practitioners of Judaism). However, they are not descended from the ancient Israelites, or Hebrew Israelites, the biological descendants of Abraham through Isaac and Jacob.

This clarification is both relevant and important because not a few people since Israel was declared a state have wrongly believed that the people of the new Israel represent a restoration and continuity of the ancient Israelites who are descended from Jacob. This, however, is not the truth as the true Israelites have remained "lost" since being expelled from the land to this day. These descendants of ancient Israelites are also dark-skinned (or black) as opposed to their light-skinned modern-day Jewish counterparts.

Incidentally, as Israel's historiography reveals, even the returnee ethnic "Jews" who came back home to Judah from exile would themselves subsequently be expelled from Judah never again to return to the land, to this day. During the Hellenistic Classical Period, Judah was absorbed into the subsequent Hellenistic kingdoms that followed the conquests of Alexander the Great, but in the second century BC, a new kingdom, the Hasmonean Kingdom, was created following a Judean revolt against the Seleucid Empire. But then, the Hasmonean Kingdom, the last nominally independent kingdom of Israel, gradually lost its independence from 63 BC with its conquest by Pompey of Rome, becoming a Roman and later

Parthian client kingdom. Following the installation of client kingdoms under the Herodian dynasty, the Province of Judea witnessed a series of civil disturbances, which culminated in the First Jewish-Roman War, and the destruction of the historic Second Temple in c.70 AD by an army led by Titus. After The Third Jewish-Roman War of 135 AD, the Romans expelled the remnant Judeans from the region and renamed it Palestine.

Biblical records of this later and final expulsion of the Israelite remnants from Judah, if any existed, were either destroyed or are yet to be rediscovered. As such, we can only speculate regarding the places these last Israelite exiles could have fled to following their expulsion from Judah.

A PEOPLE SCATTERED

"Lost Tribes" is commonly used in the contemporary period to refer to the people of Israel, but, as the term Jews is in reference to all descendants of Israel, this is a gross misnomer because Israelites were not annihilated in history and so are not lost. If they are lost indeed, then they are "lost" within existing populations across the world, where their ancestors could have migrated to after their successive expulsions from Israel, who could have assimilated them. While it would be a hugely difficult task attempting to retrace the actual migration of the ancient Israelites in order to identify each of their descendants today, it is not entirely impossible to identify possible locations across the world where their descendants could possibly exist. Some scholars have done extensive research about current global populations with Israelite ancestry, notable amongst which is

Dr. Rudolph R. Windsor, who detailed his findings in his book, *From Babylon to Timbuktu: A History of the Ancient Black Races Including the Black Hebrews,* which was originally published in 1969. The Hebrew Bible provides information relating to the possible location of Israelite descendants today in Isaiah 11: *Then it will happen on that day that the Lord Will again acquire with His hand a second time The remnant of His people, who will remain, From Assyria, from [Lower] Egypt, from Pathros, from Cush (Ethiopia), from Elam [in Persia], from Shinar [Babylonia], from Hamath [in Aram], And from the coastlands bordering the [Mediterranean] Sea* (verse 11 AMP). Some of the named locations correspond to places in previously referenced passages of the Hebrew Bible where ancient Israelites are recorded to have been expelled to. It is thus reasonable to assume that these people could subsequently have migrated further into neighbouring places in the broader regions, including the parts of Africa listed in the latest reference.

The key thing here is not to establish a full list of current ethnicities with an Israelite ancestry but to identify their possible geographical regions. Based on biblical and other records, Africa, including today's Middle East, is the place where these Israelite descendants were heavily located by about the second century AD. Other historic events, particularly historic slavery, would subsequently result in scattering these Israelite descendants across the world, especially Europe, and North and South America, while other relatively recent migrations could have helped spread them further into almost every region of the world.

CHAPTER FIVE

Jacob's Trouble

Locating the "lost" descendants of Israel in Africa and its
surroundings is very revealing and important because it helps to
better understand how and why the fortunes of Africa
subsequently changed with time. The presence of Israelites in
Africa is attested to by various discoveries in the region,
including old maps showing a "Kingdom of Judah" somewhere in
western Africa. Some ethnic groups in Africa, including the Igbo
people of Southeastern Nigeria and Akan people of Ghana, have
proven Israelite ancestry and share customs and traditions
similar to those of ancient Israelites. For instance, the eight-day
circumcision of male children, marriage and burial customs of the
Igbo people are the same as those of the Israelites as recorded in
the Hebrew Bible (e.g., in the Book of Leviticus).

African historiography reveals that the vicissitudes
suffered mainly by ancient Israel and her people in history

subsequently shifted to Africa and her people sometimes after
Israelites established themselves in the continent. For instance,
the conquest and slavery which characterised Israel's checkered
history would later become characteristic features of Africa's
history after Israelites resettled in the continent. Interestingly,
the common history of Africa as told today is one heavily defined
by slavery, such that most people today wrongly assume that
historic slavery represents the beginning of the history of Africa
and her people. This has now been shown to be untrue as Africa
already had an enviable history long before the sixteenth century,
during which the transatlantic slave trade began. It is worth
noting that the practice of slavery did not start in the sixteenth
century but already existed in prehistory.

Historical evidence indicates minor instances of forms of
slavery amongst the earliest hunter-gatherers while pointing to
the invention of agriculture as being responsible for its
proliferation especially during the Neolithic Revolution. The
historiographies of ancient civilisations such as those which
existed in Egypt, Sumer, Greece, Rome, China, and India show
recorded evidence of slavery, which was also a common practice
in Mesoamerica long before the fifteenth century during which
Europeans made their first appearance in the region starting
with Christopher Columbus. The most common forms of slavery
in Mesoamerica then were war prisoners and debtors who could
not repay debts and so were compelled to work-off such debts.
For instance, in Maya society, warfare and raids were important
and common in order to source for human resources needed for
human sacrifices and the construction of religious temples. Aztec
historical sources reveal that as many as eighty-four thousand

people were sacrificed at a temple inauguration in 1487. Note that slavery was not usually hereditary in these cultures, as children born to slaves were usually born free.

In Asia, during the ancient Chinese Qin and Han dynasties, men who were sentenced to castration as a punishment for rape became eunuch slaves used for forced labour. The government also confiscated the properties of such enslaved convicts, and their families were also subjected to enslavement. Likewise, Muslim conquests in the Indian subcontinent, starting in the eighth century but mainly from the twelfth to the sixteenth centuries, resulted in the enslavement of parts of local populations by their conquerors. Accounts of slavery and slave trade in the then India during the eleventh century was recorded by Arab historian Al-Tuba detailing the capture of some one hundred thousand youths by the armies of Mahmud of Ghazi, who was reported to have returned with such a large number of slaves enough to cause a drastic reduction in their selling price, leading to an influx of slave merchants from distant cities into the region of his domain in modern-day Central Asia.

Records of slavery in Ancient Greece go as far back as Mycenaean Greece, with slavery becoming an important aspect of the economy and society with the establishment of cities. It is estimated that in Athens, most citizens owned at least one slave, with slavery regarded as both natural and a necessity. The ancient Romans who inherited the institution of slavery from the Greeks and the Phoenicians, during the outward expansion of the Republic, enslaved entire populations from across Europe and the Mediterranean. Such slaves were used mainly as labourers in farms, quarries, and households of the elites, and also for

entertainment purposes. Roman sources account for ownership of slaves among Celtic tribes, while the Vikings also enslaved people on the British Isles and parts of Eastern Europe. The Viking slave trade slowly came to an end in the eleventh century as the Vikings began to settle in the European territories they once raided, merging with the local populace. Capture in war, voluntary
servitude, and debt slavery were common within the British Isles before 1066. Slaves were routinely bought and sold, but the trade was not a major economic factor in the British Isles during this period. Ireland and Denmark provided markets for captured Anglo-Saxon and Celtic slaves as it was common practice for slaves to run away from their owners.

Historical sources also account for the existence of slavery in different parts of Oceania: Mäore tribes in New Zealand kept war prisoners as slaves, who remained as such unless subsequently released, ransomed, or used for sacrifice. In this instance, with some exceptions, the child of a slave was also a slave. Hawaii, in ancient times, operated a now abolished social caste system where the outcast class, known as "Kauwa," believed to have been war captives or their descendants, were treated as slaves.

The practice of slavery also, already existed in Africa before the fifteenth century. Different forms of servitude and slavery were common across Africa in ancient times, as they were across parts of the ancient world, including debt slavery and enslavement of prisoners of war and convicted criminals. There was also the practice of the social caste system in some parts of Africa, resulting in the outcast class being treated as slaves. Slaves were often used in royal courts and households, for military purposes, and also for farming and other labour-intensive enterprises.

Trading of slaves was also common practice throughout Africa even before contact was made with people from the Mediterranean, notably Phoenicians, Greeks, Romans, and later, Arabs. Roman and Arab slave trades were the first major intercontinental slavery of historic proportion to affect Africa. Although Africa had been involved in trading slaves with people from outside the continent in earlier historical periods, the involvement with the Greeks and then the Romans took slave trade in the continent to historic proportions, with the Roman trade exerting more impact than the former. This was soon followed by the Arab slave trade, which extended across the Sahara Desert and across the Indian Ocean, and subsequently contributed slaves to the transatlantic trade. Some historians claim that about five million Africans were transported as slaves via the Red Sea, Indian Ocean, and Sahara Desert to other parts of the world between 1500 and 1900 as a result of the Arab slave trade.

Transatlantic slave trade, which occurred from the fifteenth century until the nineteenth century, became the culmination of historic slavery in Africa, greatly outpacing every past instance of slavery anywhere in the world. Transatlantic slavery was notorious for the following reasons: its proportion, level of inhumanity, and its commercial nature. The scale and proportion of transatlantic slavery remain unequalled, with a very conservative estimate of about ten to twelve million victims of African descent. The degree of inhumanity that characterised it is also unrivalled in addition to the fact victims were not prisoners of war, convicted criminals, or debtors, as was often the case in other past instances of slavery, but they were simply ordinary people who were forcefully abducted. Lastly, the commercial gains from transatlantic slavery was not an economic by-product but instead the main reason behind it as it was occasioned as a primary source of revenue. It would also subsequently be misapplied as a defining criterion in the history of Africa and Africans in addition to inspiring the colour-based concept of racial categorisation.

Transatlantic Slavery

Transatlantic slavery is considered an aspect of Jacob's Trouble—the various vicissitudes and persecutions of Israelites—because its victims were mainly descendants of ancient Israel who had relocated to Africa long before it started, following the expulsion from their homeland in ancient Israel, as already noted. The vast majority of those who were enslaved and transported in the transatlantic slave trade were people from Central and West Africa—a region of Africa mostly settled by ancient Israelite migrants. Research has shown that those Africans who arrived in the US as enslaved persons came mainly from the coasts of West Africa, with high numbers taken from Senegambia, West-Central Africa, Ghana, Ivory Coast, Togo, Benin Republic, Nigeria, and Cameroon. It is worth noting that the numbers shipped to the US represented only about 3.6 percent of the total number of people taken from Africa as enslaved persons. A greater proportion of victims were transported to the island-colonies in the Caribbean, other colonies in North America (apart from the USA), colonies in South America (notably Brazil), and countries in Europe (notably Britain, France, Spain, and Portugal). Additionally, there are other specific characteristics of transatlantic slavery that not only contributed to set it apart from all other instances of slavery but also closely resemble past instances of slavery as exclusively suffered by ancient Israelites.

For this purpose, we shall refer to the Hebrew Bible but first note that the main reason behind the conquest of the Kingdom of Israel and subsequently the Kingdom of Judah was disobedience to God and effectively a breach in the covenant made by God with Abraham. Deuteronomy 28 gives a detailed list of the blessings and curses associated with this covenant, with the list of curses starting from the fifteenth verse. The following is recorded in subsequent verses: *Because you did not serve the LORD your God with a heart full of joy and gladness for the abundance of all things [with which He blessed you], you will therefore serve your enemies whom the LORD sends against you, in hunger and in thirst, in nakedness and in lack of all things; and He will put an* **iron yoke** *[of slavery]* **on your neck** *until He has destroyed you. "The LORD will bring* **a nation against you from far away**, *from the end of the earth, [as swift] as the eagle swoops down [to attack],* **a nation whose language you will not understand**, *a defiant nation who will have no respect for the old, nor show favor to the young* (Deuteronomy 28: 47–50 AMP). Although history reveals that some past instances of slavery involved the enslavement of particular groups of people by foreigners, this was particularly the case with all instances of the enslavement of ancient Israelites, who were severally enslaved by Assyrians, Babylonians, Persians and Medes, Greeks, and

Romans. Perhaps ancient Israelites are the only people to have suffered enslavement in different historical periods by the greatest number of different foreign nationals. While the exact nature of Israel's past enslavement is not detailed in available records, several features of transatlantic slavery correspond very closely to every condition specified in the curses listed in the referenced text, including "an iron yoke on your neck," "a nation from far away whose language you will not understand," and "a defiant nation with no respect for the old nor show favour to the young." More punitive conditions are given in Deuteronomy 28 as follows: *You will be **pledged to marry a wife, but another man will be intimate with her** [before you]; you **will build a house, but you will not live in it**; you **will plant a vineyard, but you will not use its fruit**. Your ox will be slaughtered before your eyes, but you will not eat any of it; your donkey will be torn away from you, and it will not be returned to you; your sheep will be given to your enemies, and you will have no one to save you. **Your sons and daughters will be given to another people**, while your eyes look on and long for them continually; but there will be nothing you can do. **You will have sons and daughters, but they will not be yours** [for long], because they will go into captivity* (Deuteronomy 28: 30–32; 41 AMP). This also was particularly the case with transatlantic slavery during which spouses were forcefully separated from each other and wives raped by slave owners or traders, enslaved persons were used in the construction of houses which they were not permitted to live in, they cultivated crops which they were not allowed to eat, and had children who were forcefully removed from them and sold into further slavery. Most of all, they were not able to do anything in response.

The curses continue: *And the LORD **will scatter you among all the nations, from one end of the earth to the other; and there you will [be forced to] serve other gods,** [lifeless gods of] wood and stone, which neither you nor your fathers have known. **Among those nations you will find no peace** (rest), and there will be no resting place for the sole of your foot; but there the LORD will give you a trembling heart, failing eyes, and a despairing soul. Your life will hang in doubt before you; night and day you will be filled with anxiety and have no assurance of living. In the morning you will say, 'I wish it were evening!' and in the evening you will say, 'I wish it were morning!'—because of the dread in your heart with which you tremble, and because of the sight of your eyes which you will see* (Deuteronomy 28: 64–67 AMP). History accounts for the scattering of the African victims of transatlantic slavery across the world, particularly Europe and North and South America. It is known that slavery resulted in the presence of some black populations with recent African origin in the Caribbean, parts of Europe, and North and South America. A number of victims were also forcefully converted into different local religions, notably Christianity and Islam. (Before transatlantic slavery began, some of the Israelites who had escaped to Africa following their conquest and expulsion from Israel had with time already resorted to various forms of idolatry upon arriving in Africa, although history accounts for different ethnic groups in Africa who practiced the Israelite system of religious worship before the advent of transatlantic slavery.). Likewise, victims of transatlantic slavery lived mainly in fear and uncertainty, not knowing if or when they would be sold, resold, or killed.

It would not be necessary to present a comprehensive

account of the cruelty and ignominy which characterised transatlantic slavery in this book, nor would it have been easy. However, such information already exists in various publications narrating the experiences of enslaved persons during this particular incidence of slavery, with some of them written by formerly enslaved persons. The following is a few recommended list: *The Frederick Douglas Papers, Series 2: Autobiographical Writings, Vol. 1: Narrative* (1845) and *My Bondage and My Freedom* (1855) by Frederick Douglas; *Narrative of the Life of Frederick Douglas, an American Slave* (1845) by Zarie Williams; *Incidents in the Life of a Slave Girl* (1861) by Harriet Ann Jacobs; *The Interesting Narrative of the Life of Olaudah Equiano* (1789) by Olaudah Equiano; *Fifty years in chains* (1837) by Charles Ball; *Narrative of Sojourner Truth* (1850) by Sojourner Truth; *Twelve Years a Slave* (1853) by Solomon Northup; *The Half Has Never Been Told: Slavery and the Making of American Capitalism* (2014) by Edward E. Baptist; *Roots: The Saga of an American family* (1976) by Alex Haley; and *Uncle Tom's Cabin* (1852) by Harriet Beecher Stowe.

In Equiano's book, *The Interesting Narrative of the Life of Olaudah Equiano*, he writes about his abduction, which took place in about 1753 at a very young age of about seven or eight years: *One day when all our people were gone out to their works as usual, and only I and my dear sister were left to mind the house, two men and a woman got over our walls, and in a moment seized us both; and, without giving us time to cry out, or make resistance, they stopped our mouths, and ran off with us into the nearest wood. Here they tied our hands, and continued to carry us as far as they could, till night came on, when we reached a small house, where the robbers halted for refreshment, and spent the night.* In the midst of their predicament, the only source of little comfort for Olaudah and his sister was the company they had of each other, but even they were soon deprived of both, as his narration continues: *The next day proved a day of greater sorrow than I had yet experienced; for my sister and I were then separated, while we lay clasped in each other's arms. It was in vain that we besought them not to part us; she was torn from me, and immediately carried away, while I was left in a state of distraction not to be described. I cried and grieved continually; and for several days did not eat anything but what they forced into my mouth.* Lives were instantly disrupted, families torn apart, and a hapless and hopeless existence in enslavement commenced.

Another gruesome aspect of transatlantic slavery relates to the actual transportation of enslaved persons including the conditions under which they are held pending shipment. Victims were often transported to various coastal ports where they would be held in large forts called "factories." Notable slave forts in Africa included those found in Benguela (in Angola), Elmina and Cape Coasts (in Ghana), Bonny (in Nigeria), and Bunce Island (in Sierra Leone). A visit to any of the surviving forts in these ports would reveal the squalid and subhuman conditions under which enslaved people were made to live pending subsequent sale to other traders and transportation across the Atlantic. Historian and author Milton Meltzer writes in his book, *Slavery: A World History* (1993) that about 4.5 percent of deaths associated with the transatlantic slave trade took place during this phase, thus demonstrating the gruesomeness of life in a transatlantic slave factory. The "factory phase" was followed by the infamous

"Middle Passage", the phase of the triangular trade involving ports in Africa, Europe and the Americas during which slaves were forcibly transported to the Americas. This phase was characterised by further brutal treatment and poor care, with slaves crammed into tight, unsanitary spaces for prolonged periods of up to several months, with limited access to fresh air and exercise. Records show that ships were fitted with between three hundred and fifty to six hundred enslaved passengers in the compartment designed for holding enslaved persons in the basement. There were also instances of enforced dehumanising "showers" (as bathing) and "dancing" (as exercise) above deck occasionally, as well as force-feeding of enslaved persons who preferred to starve to death instead of living as slaves. A significant number are known to have jumped overboard, driven by misery and inhuman treatment. The spread of fatal diseases was also common due to the deplorable conditions on board. Meltzer's estimate places the mortality rate during this phase at 12.5 percent.

Olaudah Equiano, in his narrative, also gives a descriptive account of his experience during this phase. Regarding the lower deck of the ship he was being transported in, he writes: *The stench of the hold while we were on the coast was so intolerably loathsome, that it was dangerous to remain there for any time, and some of us had been permitted to stay on the deck for fresh air; but now that the whole ship's cargo was confined together, it became absolutely pestilential. The closeness of the place, and the heat of the climate, added to the number in the ship, which was so crowded that each had scarcely room to turn himself, almost suffocated us. This produced copious perspirations, so that the air soon became unfit for respiration, from a variety of loathsome smells, and brought on a sickness among the slaves, of which many died, thus falling victims to the improvident avarice, as I may call it, of their purchasers. This wretched situation was again aggravated by the galling of the chains, now become insupportable, and the filth of the necessary tubs [sanitary buckets], into which the children often fell, and were almost suffocated. The shrieks of the women, and the groans of the dying, rendered the whole a scene of horror almost inconceivable.*

Another personal account referencing the middle passage was from Ali Eisami from Kanuri, in Northern Nigeria, who was abducted sometime in 1818 but was luckily rescued while being transported to the Americas and later taken to Sierra Leone. His recollection of life aboard the slave ship includes the following, recorded in a short memoir of his enslavement by the German missionary Sigismund Koelle: *The people of the great vessel were wicked: when we had been shipped, they took away all the small pieces of cloth which were on our bodies, and threw them into the water, then they took chains and fettered two together. We in the vessel, young and old, were seven hundred, whom the White men had bought. We were all fettered round our feet, and all the oldest died of thirst, for there was no water. Every morning they had to take many, and throw them into the water.*

Furthermore, upon eventually arriving at their destination, those enslaved persons who survived the gruesome Middle Passage were further subjected to more inhuman treatments. In the Americas, new arrivals were often subjected to "seasoning." Seasoning camps were prominent throughout the Caribbean where freshly-arrived enslaved persons were subjected to some form of conditioning in order to break them, thus ensuring full servitude and compliance, which naturally involved brutality, torture and physical violence. Environmental and climatic factors coupled with violence and torture, led to a huge number of deaths upon arrival. Meltzer estimates that about thirty-three percent of new arrivals would have died within their first year at these camps. The final phase of enslavement, during which slaves were condemned to a life of one form of servitude or another, was pretty much as gruesome as any of the preceding phases, if not even worse in some cases. Living conditions were squalid, working hours unnecessarily long and unhealthy, daily quotas (for some jobs such as cotton picking) were unreasonably high while failure to meet with quotas attracted severe punishment, including flogging; female slaves were randomly subjected to sexual violence, including frequently being raped, while some men and boys were sodomised; children were forcibly separated from their mothers and sold on to new owners, marriage among slaves was not permitted except in rare cases and usually for the economic benefit of slave owners, slaves were spontaneously uprooted from settled locations to new locations without notice thereby further unsettling them emotionally and otherwise; others were subjected to savagery, in order to subdue them, while some who were unsuccessful in their escape bids were summarily executed to serve as a warning and deterrent to the others; life was uncertain, and hope was nonexistent.

The personal account of Mary Prince, a young girl born into slavery and enslaved in the West Indies, in her book, *The History of Mary Prince, A West Indian Slave* (1831), sheds some light on some aspects of life during the final phase of enslavement. Narrating her experience in the hands of her second master, she gave an account of what is obviously a form of sexual abuse: *He had an ugly fashion of stripping himself quite naked, and ordering me then to wash him in a tub of water. This was worse to me than all the licks [flogging]. Sometimes when he called me to wash him I would not come, my eyes were so full of shame. He would then come to beat me. One time I had plates and knives in my hand, and I dropped both plates and knives, and some of the plates were broken. He struck me so severely for this, that at last I defended myself, for I thought it was high time to do so.* About a former mistress, Mary writes: *The next morning my mistress set about instructing me in my tasks. She taught me to do all sorts of household work; to wash and bake, pick cotton and wool, and wash floors, and cook. And she taught me (how can I ever forget it!) more things than these; she caused me to know the exact difference between the smart of the rope, the cart-whip, and the cow-skin, when applied to my naked body by her own cruel hand. And there was scarcely any punishment more dreadful than the blows I received on my face and head from her hard heavy fist. She was a fearful woman, and a savage mistress to her slaves.*

Mary's account about the day she was to be sold from the household where she was born a slave describes the agony of a mother and the misery of her children as both were being separated, in some cases for life: *The black morning at length came; it came too soon for my poor mother and us. Whilst she was putting on us the new osnaburgs in which we were to be sold, she said, in a sorrowful voice, (I shall never forget it!) 'See, I am shrouding my poor children; what a task for a mother!' ⏶ She then called Miss Betsey to take leave of us. 'I am going to carry my little chickens to market,' (these were her words,) 'take your last look of them; may be you will see them no more'. The [other] slaves could say nothing to comfort us; they could only weep and lament with us. When I left my dear little brothers and the house in which I had been brought up, I thought my heart would burst.* The true and full story of transatlantic slavery could never be told, but it is unarguably the worst instance of slavery in human history and will never be equalled or rivalled.

Finally, related to the curses listed in Deuteronomy, this is also recorded: *Because you did not obey the voice of the LORD your God, you who were as numerous as the stars of heaven shall be left few in number* (Deuteronomy 28: 62 AMP). The ancient Israelite population was severally severely decimated at different historical periods as a result of warfare and conquest while transatlantic slavery also saw to a drastic reduction in their surviving numbers (now living in Africa) as many victims were either killed or died in the process of abduction and transportation, and for some others, during their enslavement. A source from the BBC News reported that approximately 1.2 to 2.4 million Africans died in transit as they were being transported outside Africa while more are estimated to have died soon upon arrival at their respective destinations. The number of lives lost in the procurement of slaves, which presently is still unknown and include those killed during raids or while trying to escape capture, contributes to the overall toll. It is estimated that this number may equal or exceed the number who survived to be enslaved.

Dispassionate scrutiny of different features of transatlantic slavery reveals that it is unique in several ways and that it is not like any other past instances of slavery. Comparing these unique features with several biblical curses associated with

God's covenant with Abraham show a close similarity too difficult to be ignored or which could be simply attributed to coincidence.

Transatlantic slavery, although now relegated to history, continues to negatively impact its main victims—black people of modern African descent—in various other ways, both directly and indirectly. Transatlantic slavery is mainly responsible for the colour-based racial categorisation models and the subsequent racialisation of some ethnic populations, particularly black. The ideology of race was conceived starting from the seventeenth century but became more pervasive and biased during the nineteenth century, following the abolition of slavery, resulting in the wrong assumption that "races" were primordial, natural, enduring, and distinct. At the peak of transatlantic slavery late in the eighteenth century, polygenism was advocated in England by historian Edward Long and anatomist Charles White, in Germany by ethnographers Christoph Meiners and Georg Forster, and in France by anthropologist Julien-Joseph Virey. Polygenism argues for an independent regional evolution of humans and that populations in different regions shared no common ancestors. The doctrine was later promoted in the US by natural scientist Samuel George Morton, physician and surgeon Josiah Nott, and biologist and geologist Louis Agassiz in the middle of the nineteenth century.

Eugenism soon followed polygenism late in the nineteenth century and was initially used to effectively advance the idea of racial superiority before being expanded later, early in the twentieth century, to advocate for the existence of a "pure race" within the white race. It seems then that soon after slavery was abolished, some scholars of European descent deemed it necessary to isolate its main victims—black people—while reclassifying them as a separate race different and inferior to their self-appointed white race. Thus, the origin of the racial inequality which has plagued the global modern society till this day. In the US, for instance, the abolition of slavery was instantly followed with racial segregation, which in some states was backed by laws, as well as with various other forms of racial discrimination, including denial of equal rights, lynching and wanton destruction of properties. Furthermore, transatlantic slavery has also been misapplied as a defining criterion for the identity and history of black people with modern African descent which in turn is largely responsible for the inaccurate and incomplete history in public domain.

Finally, and sadly, transatlantic slavery has also been used to foster divisions among its main victims as people with a common ancestry have become polarised through incomplete and inaccurate historical narratives. Black Africans in North and South America, including the Caribbean, have in the past exhibited some degree of mistrust against those in Africa because of what they have been told regarding the role played by the ancestors of the latter group in selling their own ancestors into slavery. Likewise, different ethnic groups in Africa continue to mistrust each other due to a history related to transatlantic slavery. Whatever be the truth regarding these accusations, which have resulted in acrimony, it is sad that these people now demonstrate disunity eerily similar to that which existed in the divided kingdoms of ancient Israel. And mainly due to transatlantic slavery and some stories associated with it.

Colonisation

The colonisation of Africa is very similar to transatlantic slavery in that, like the latter, it was unique in many ways when compared to other forms of colonisation in known history; whereas other instances of colonisation subsequently came to an end, the colonisation of Africa has continued in other forms long after it was officially ended, and, the impact and consequences of the colonisation of Africa remain unrivalled including the near-total destruction of indigenous ways and cultures which were forcefully replaced with supposedly superior Western alternatives. An equally significant point here is that the historic colonisation of Africa also occurred only after descendants of ancient Israel resettled in the region. Although the ancient Greek, and subsequently, Romans, conquered ancient Egypt in an earlier period, the extent of that colonisation was very limited in comparison to the latter colonisation in Africa, which started from the nineteenth century, during which almost all of Africa was colonised. Like slavery, Africa's past history of colonisation has become a major factor in the subsequent definition of both the identity and history of Africa and her people; Africans continue to be treated around the world as subjects of former colonial powers while Africa's affairs remain heavily influenced by her former colonisers. Although colonisation is officially ended in Africa, with the granting of state independence to former colonies, what African nation-states have is "flag independence" but not real autonomy as Africa continues to be dominated and controlled through neocolonialism. This is a very unique and important point because, as noted, it sets the colonisation of Africa apart from other instances of colonisation in known history.

Colonisation is derived from the Latin word *colere*, meaning "to inhabit." Colonisation is the process through which a political entity (e.g., kingdom, empire, or nation-state) forcibly establishes settlements in lands belonging to another political entity while also dominating the latter entity politically and otherwise. Theoretically, colonisation started with the foremost human ancestors who had originated in Africa and subsequently colonised the rest of the world. For instance, in the old Americas, historiography reveals that the Olmec civilisation had emerged in Mesoamerica as early as around 1600 BC as a predecessor to the other historic civilisations in the region, notably Maya and Aztec. From around 250 AD, the Mayan civilisation developed a large number of city-states linked by a complex trade network and existed as a dominant force in the region. Its decline during the ninth century saw the rise of Chichen Itza in the north of the Mayan region and the aggressive expansion of the K'iche kingdom of Q'umarkaj in the Guatemalan Highlands. From about 1300 AD, the Aztec civilisation arose in Mesoamerica, in what is now central Mexico, which was once part of the domain of the Mayan civilisation. Thus, the Aztec colonised some areas which were previously Mayan territory. The whole of the old Americas would subsequently come under European colonisation starting from the fifteenth century; the Spanish Empire colonised most of the Americas from the southwest of today's US, Florida and the Caribbean to the southern tip of South America. The Portuguese on their part, colonised most of Brazil while the British colonised the eastern coast of the US, the North Pacific coast, and most parts of Canada. The French also colonised Quebec, parts of Eastern Canada, and parts of Central US, while the Dutch colonised New York, some islands in the Caribbean and parts of Northern South America. The US, Canada, Brazil, and other countries in the region subsequently became independent, remaining so until date.

In the old Eurasia, archaeology has shown that today's Southeast Asia and Southern Europe were first settled by dark-skinned migrants from Africa, while Northcentral Asia and Northern Europe had light-skinned earlier settlers. The historiography of Eurasia reveal that the earlier Proto-Indo-European settlers in Northern Europe were succeeded by the Indo-Iranian who, from around 1800 BC colonised a greater part of the region, including the Caucasus, Central Asia, the Indian sub-continent, and the Iranian Plateau. Before the Indo-Iranian expansion across the Indian sub-continent, other indigenous civilisations already existed in the region, such as the Indus Valley (or Harappa), the earliest known of these civilisations, which at its peak had an estimate of more than five million inhabitants and over a thousand urban cities. Its earliest beginning is dated to c. 3300 BC. From about 1500 BC, the Indo-Iranian expansion began resulting in the rise of the Vedic civilisation, which colonised parts of the Indian sub-continent. The Mahajanapadas kingdoms rose in the region from the sixth century BC and were succeeded by different empires, including Nanda, Maurya, Shunga, and Kanva. During the thirteenth century, the Turkic people of Central Asia colonised parts of the Indian subcontinent establishing the Delhi Sultanate in 1206. The Mongol who founded the Mughal (or Mogul) Empire in 1526 also colonised parts of the sub-continent during the sixteenth century. The Portuguese, Dutch, British, and the French were part of the European powers to colonise different parts of the Indian subcontinent starting from the fifteenth century.

In the European side of old Eurasia, the Proto-Indo-Europeans who first settled the northern region subsequently spread east, and by early in the second millennium BC had expanded across Anatolia, the Aegean, and Central Asia. In Mediterranean Europe, the Minoan civilisation was founded around 2600 BC by Africans, in ancient Greece, before the Indo-Iranian expansion during the second millennium BC gave cause to the Mycenaean civilisation around 1600 BC (and also the Hyksos dynasty in ancient Egypt in 1640 BC). Ancient Rome rose in the region during the eighth century, succeeding ancient Greek civilisations as the dominant force in the region and subsequently colonising a broader region which included Egypt, in Africa, and a vast part of Europe, including today's Britain, Greece, France, Spain, Portugal, Hungary, Romania, Turkey, and parts of Germany. Ancient Rome's colonisation of Europe came to an end following Hunnic and Germanic migration across Europe, starting from the fourth and fifth centuries respectively, resulting in former Roman colonies being taken over by Germanic and Hunnic peoples. Of these Germanic peoples, the Franks founded the Barbarian kingdom of Francia (or Kingdom of the Franks), from which France and Germany later emerged; while the Angles and Saxons (later merged into Anglo-Saxon), together with the indigenous Celtic Britons, founded different kingdoms such as Kent, East Anglia, Wessex, Mercia, and Northumbria, from which England would subsequently emerge.

The point of the foregoing is to demonstrate that colonisation is integral to the history of every region or continent of the world and existed starting from prehistory; and so it is not quite an African thing as current attitudes seem to suggest. What is true though, is that the colonisation of Africa stands out from every other instance of colonisation for the reasons earlier stated.

The colonisation of Africa constitutes an aspect of Jacob's Trouble because it only affected Africa after ancient Israelites had migrated to the region, thus becoming part of the total victims. To demonstrate this, we shall again refer to the Hebrew Bible, in Deuteronomy 28. Regarding the exploitation of natural and other resources, this is recorded: ***A people whom you do not know will eat the produce of your land and all the products of your labors***, *and you will never be anything but oppressed and exploited and crushed continually. You shall be driven mad by the sight of the things you see. and it will eat the offspring of your herd and the produce of your ground until you are destroyed, who will leave you no grain, new wine, or oil, nor the offspring of your herd or the young of your flock until they have caused you to perish.* ***They will besiege you in all your cities until your high and fortified walls in which you trusted come down*** *throughout your land; and they will besiege you in all your cities throughout your land which the LORD your God has given you.* (Deuteronomy 28: 33–34; 51–52 AMP). It is instructive to note that although different parts of Africa had in the past been colonised by other Africans; for instance, the Bantu expansion, which resulted in the present dominance of the Bantu in the whole of Africa; it was the subsequent colonisation of Africa by foreigners (Europeans) that greatly impacted her irreparably, including the exploitation of her resources which continues until date. Interestingly, the degree of resource exploitation and expropriation, which characterised the conquest and colonisation of ancient Israel in ancient times by Assyrians, Babylonians, Medes and Persians, Greeks, and Romans, would subsequently characterise the colonisation of Africa during the nineteenth and twenty centuries. Continuing long after colonisation was supposed to have ended. The continued exploitation of Africa, through neo-colonialism, eerily resonates with the, *and you will never be anything but oppressed and exploited and crushed continually*, contained in the curses. It is appropriate to note here that the "Scramble for Africa," which resulted in her colonisation, was motivated primarily for economic, political, and social reasons.

The rapid industrialisation resulting from the Second Industrial Revolution (or the Technological Revolution), late in the nineteenth century—in 1870; the First Industrial Revolution occurred between 1760 and 1820 or 1840—brought with it a worldwide price and economic recession starting from 1873, known historically as the Long Depression. The recession was most severe in Western Europe and North America. The resultant balance of trade deficit made it very necessary for the affected countries in Europe to seek an external trade market that could guarantee a trade surplus—a market that bought more from them than it sold to them. Africa presented an excellent and easy target, colonised, it would become more easily manageable. Additionally, political rivalry between leading European countries was another factor for colonisation of Africa; different trading empires sought control of key waterways that linked the Eastern and Western Hemispheres, both for trading and military purposes, including the acquisition of overseas military and naval bases. More so, colonies were also seen as assets in the balance of power negotiations, useful as items of exchange at times of international bargaining, as well as sources for military power represented by local populations who could be used as soldiers. Finally, colonisation was motivated for social reasons, including the need to resettle surplus populations in Europe as the prevailing economic recession made the provision of decent social amenities such as housing and welfare facilities very difficult. Also, the rapid industrialisation led to high unemployment rates as people were replaced by machines leading to an explosion of social problems like crime and civil protests.

Having noted economic factors as part of the motivation behind the colonisation of Africa, the manipulation of her resources would become a significant aspect of her colonisation. Consequently, her local personal and corporate economies suffered greatly as a result of colonial economic policies. Precolonial local economies in Africa were mostly rural-based, consisting mainly of agriculture and agro-based activities with individual economies consisting primarily of food crop production, grown primarily for local consumption, while the corporate or communal economy was centred around the production of cash crops which were grown mainly for export within and outside Africa. Although it was common for some individuals to also cultivate cash crops, howbeit on a secondary basis. Colonisation resulted in a common policy of forced cultivation and expanded operations through which local farmers were induced to grow and expand their outputs of those export commodities needed in Europe—such as cocoa, cotton, rubber, oil palm, and tobacco—to feed the demand of industrialisation. This enforced cultivation also violated some indigenous cultural practices, some of which were used to ensure that balance in the ecosystem was maintained, and others that were sacred and served religious purposes. Farmers were required in some cases to grow crops, which in their custom was a taboo, and also to cultivate lands which were sacred and not to be cultivated. Additionally, trading was no longer conducted in a free and fair open market but was taken over by the European powers who strictly regulated it in order to guard their interest, oftentimes through the use of European merchant-firms—such as the African and Eastern Trade Corporation and Royal Niger Company (which merged later to become United Africa Company), and John Holt and Company. These European merchant-firms subjected local African farmers to exploitative relationships. In addition to helping to impoverish local people, the agricultural policies adopted by European powers during colonisation resulted in food shortages, thus beginning Africa's history of poverty and famine. Furthermore, another significant aspect of colonial economic policies in Africa involved the mining of mineral resources. Consequently, a significant proportion of the local labour force was diverted from other economic ventures into the exploration of minerals at a huge loss to Africa in terms of human and natural resources. The forestry policy adopted as a result also resulted in deforestation as timber logging was en-couraged and unregulated, and forest reserves and other lands reserved for other economic and development activities were randomly violated and excavated in search of minerals.

Lives, many lives, were also lost in the process. A historic example is the "Congo Horrors" which occurred in the Belgian colony of Congo Free State during the reign of King Leopold II of Belgium. The labour policies used by Belgium for the collection of natural rubber in the colony for export resulted in an estimated total loss of between one to fifteen million local people, including those who died as a result of disease and famine. A local paramilitary unit, the Force Publique, set up to enforce labour policies could kill anyone who failed to participate in the collection of rubber or to adhere to any of the policies. Notable abuses include the severing of hands of victims who fell short of the state policy and burning of villages. A slave-labour system, known as the "Red Rubber system," was also employed as labour was demanded by the colonial administration as taxation.

Added to the past destruction of Africa's economy through colonial strategies, which ensured her peoples were reduced to poverty despite their wealth of natural resources, is the current exploitation of Africa's natural resources through neocolonial strategies, which ensures her people remain in poverty. Africa is richly blessed with an enormous wealth of natural resources, including vast deposits of minerals (e.g., diamonds, gold, silver, tantalum, uranium, bauxite), petroleum, agricultural produce (e.g., cocoa, oil palm, groundnuts, cotton, tea, tobacco), and trees. However, none of her countries is in direct or full control of their resources. Mining and exploration in all cases are signed over to foreign companies, particularly in the so-called global West (e.g., the US, Canada, UK, France, and Germany), whose modus operandi ensure that most of the economic value and revenue realised in the process go to their home nations. Exploration in Nigeria (Africa's largest oil and gas producer), which dates back to around the early-twentieth century, is largely controlled by Shell (British-Dutch), Chevron (USA), Exxon-Mobil (USA), Agip (Italian), and Total (France) even though each company now operates in a joint venture with the Nigerian National Petroleum Corporation (NNPC). Mining in The Democratic Republic of the Congo—which accounts for a significant proportion of the global production of cobalt, copper, diamond, tantalum, tin, and gold; and the country's largest source of export income—is also controlled by foreign corporations. In 2011, at least twenty-five international mining companies were active in the country, according to Datamonitor (a UK-based market intelligence and data analysis company). Examples of foreign mining companies presently in the country include Glencore (Anglo-Swiss), Randgold (UK), Ivanhoe (Canada), African Metals Corporation (Canada), and Lundin Mining Corporation (Canada). This arrangement, which is repeated across the continent, generates riches for some African elites and vastly more for the foreign prospectors but offer little to Africa and a vast majority of her people. Consequently, Africa remains poor amidst her wealth of resources, as her resources are exploited for the benefit of her exploiters, mainly in the West.

Similarly, relating to the curses in Deuteronomy, almost all of Africa's historic fortresses and cities were conquered and torn down in the pursuit of her colonisation. Following her conquest, Africa was partitioned among her conquerors thus: Belgium got the Congo Free State, Belgian Congo (today's Democratic Republic of the Congo), and Ruanda-Urundi (today's Rwanda and Burundi); France got what was known then as French West Africa (including Mauritania, Senegal, Mali, Guinea, Ivory Coast, Benin, Togo, and Niger), French Equatorial Africa (including Gabon, Republic of the Congo, Central African Republic, and part of Cameroon), French North Africa (including

Algeria, Tunisia, Morocco, and part of Egypt), and French East
Africa (including Madagascar, Djibouti, and Mauritius);
Germany got German Kamerun (now part of Cameroon and
Nigeria), German East Africa (Rwanda, Burundi, and Tanzania),
German Togoland (Togo and eastern part of Ghana), and
Namibia (known then as German South-West Africa); Italy got
Libya, Eritrea, and part of Somalia; Portugal got a share of Africa
which included Angola, Mozambique, Guinea-Bissau, and Cape
Verde; Spain got Northern and Southern Spanish Morocco, and
Spanish Sahara (Western Sahara); while Britain got a share
which included parts of Egypt and Somalia, British East Africa
(including Kenya, Uganda, and Tanzania), Botswana, Zimbabwe,
Zambia, British South Africa, and British West Africa (including
Gambia, Sierra Leone, Nigeria, British Togoland, part of
Cameroon, Ghana (known then as Gold Coast), Malawi, and
Swaziland. Even though colonisation had officially ended in
Africa by late in the twentieth century, these African countries
remain under the control of their former colonisers, who continue
to exercise significant influence in internal and external policies,
particularly political and economic. It is worth noting that the
continued exploitation of Africa is partly assisted by the manner
in which her countries were constituted by the former colonisers;
major ethnic groups were broken into different countries while
rival ethnic groups were forced together to form individual
countries, thus resulting in countries disunited by ethnic
rivalries. A classic case of divide-and-rule. For instance, in the
East Africa Protectorate (or British East Africa), from which
Kenya and Uganda were constituted, the Luo (or Joluo) people
were divided across Kenya, Uganda, and Tanzania instead of

being retained as part of a single country, while the Maasai people were also divided and shared between Kenya and Tanzania. Similarly, in Rhodesia—which was later divided into Northern Rhodesia (Zambia) and Southern Rhodesia (Zimbabwe)—two main rival ethnic groups, Shona and Ndebele, were joined together in constituting Zimbabwe. In West Africa also, Nigeria was constituted from an incongruous mix of divergent ethnic groups, including the Hausa and Fulani peoples (in the North), the Yoruba people (in the West), and the Igbo people (in the East), and also by joining together several ancient empires, such as the Bornu Empire, Sokoto Islamic Caliphate, Benin Kingdom, Kingdom of Ile-Ife, and Nri Kingdom, some of whom were rival empires before the amalgamation.

The disunity characteristic of Africa and her countries is a major reason she is yet to be free from colonial influence, while Asia presents a totally different scenario with former colonies, such as India and Pakistan, truly independent, particularly with respect to resource control.

Racism

Racism in this context goes beyond the ideology underlying the concept of race to include all forms of inequalities, unfair treatments, prejudice, discrimination, marginalisation, hate, antagonism, stereotyping, violence, abuse, and pervasive attitude by an individual, community, or institution against a person or people on the basis of their membership of a particular racial or ethnic group, particularly one that is marginalised. Based simply on this definition, it can be argued that anyone can be racist regardless of their racial group such that while a black person can suffer racism at the hands of a white person, the latter could also be a victim of racism inflicted by the former. This is true theoretically. In practice, however, it is not as simple as that. The underlying criterion in the definition of racism is the presumed superiority and inferiority of different racial groups, such that a person can only suffer racism where their racial group is generally deemed inferior. Racism is individual when it is perpetrated by an individual and is institutional or systemic when it is driven by institutional or governmental policies and practices. Although individual racism is harmful and damaging to its victims, systemic racism is the more destructive of the two. The origin of the ideology of race has previously been noted, as well as its lack of scientific validity or consensus.

Race is merely a social construct whose invention was motivated by pervasive bias and which was subsequently politicised and weaponised as a tool for the marginalisation, discrimination and unequal treatment of the people it was targeted against—Blacks. Despite its spurious origins and lack of validity, race, nonetheless, remains in wide application globally, including being used by governmental institutions and organisations. The tacit systemic support for the ideology of race and its application in racism is the main reason it is one of the biggest social problems faced in the world today.

Racism, as defined, constitutes a significant aspect of Jacob's Trouble because its primary victims include the modern-day descendants of the ancient Israelites who are now "lost" within the global black population. Furthermore, racism underlies the uniqueness of transatlantic slavery and the colonisation of Africa, as previously noted: Victims in both instances were especially so afflicted because of their racial group. Finally, the global hotbeds of racism are parts of the world with significant populations of the "lost" descendants of the ancient Israelites, particularly the US and the Caribbean, Western Europe, and parts of South America, where enslaved Africans were taken to in huge numbers during transatlantic slavery. It is instructive to note that while individual and systemic racism plague the Black Africans in the Diaspora—abroad—a different form of systemic racism is used to afflict the Black Africans in Africa—at home. The latter is represented in the neocolonialism currently being used to exploit and marginalise Africa. The curses in Deuteronomy 28 contain some specific conditions visible in the racism targeted against Black Africans, as a part of the global black population, including this: **The stranger who lives among you will rise above you higher and higher**, and you will go down lower and lower. **He will lend to you** [out of his affluence], but you will not lend to him [because of your poverty]; **he will be the head**, and you the tail. (Deuteronomy 28: 43–44 AMP).

Apartheid in Southern African countries represents a classic case of *the stranger who lives among you will rise above you higher and higher, and you will go down lower and lower* because it elevated and enriched the foreigners in the land while also subjugating and impoverishing the owners of the land. In the Republic of South Africa, under Apartheid, residents were classified into four main groups in 1950 under the Population Registration Act—Black, White, Coloured, and Indian; while racial segregation was enforced under the Groups Areas Act of 1950. The unequal nature of this segregation is evidenced in the use of the term "ghetto" in reference to some areas inhabited by various black communities in the country. The Reservation of Separate Amenities Act in 1953 was then used to enforce segregation in social facilities with amenities in public areas such as hospitals, universities, and parks clearly labelled, indicating which racial group could use what. Other legislations used in advancing apartheid in the country include the Bantu Education Act of 1953, which segregated education nationwide, and the "pass laws" used to restrict the movement of the less-privileged races in the country. The pass laws made it illegal for blacks in the country to wander into any non-Blacks areas (especially Whites-only areas) without a formal authorisation in the form of a "pass"; a type of internal passport system authorising movement to specified areas and for specified purposes. The cumulative and general impact of these discriminatory state-sponsored policies is that of richly empowering the white populace, for whom they were meant to enrich and protect, while also greatly impoverishing the black populace who were intended to be marginalised by them. The choicest opportunities, including education, careers, jobs, and accommodation and other welfare facilities, became the exclusive preserve of whites, who, as a result, became more empowered above the other races, politically, economically, and socially. Furthermore, political power and structures were dominated by whites who also ensured the status quo was maintained thereby perpetuating the marginalisation of the other races as well as making it practically impossible for them to break free from the servitude imposed on them by the unhealthy and unbalanced system which was advantageous only to the white race who instituted it.

Likewise, Africa's meteoric debt burden resonates with the, *He will lend to you, but you will not lend to him* aspect of the curse. The combined foreign debt profile of African nations is beyond reason and fails to make any iota of economic sense, especially when their wealth in natural resources is considered. Financial sources, including the World Bank, reveal the high figures owed by some of the top-ranking debtor-nations in the continent as at the end of 2017. The sums which are represented in billions and US Dollars (USD) include: South Africa (143), Angola (37.7), Ethiopia (22.5), Kenya (22.2), Ghana (21.2), Nigeria (18.91), and Tanzania (15.9). On the other hand, is the emergence of "Top Richest People in Africa," among whom are politically-connected individuals, including family members and associates of political leaders and owners of businesses who exert great influence in the corridors of power. Recent figures from Forbes Magazine, in 2018, shown in billions and USD (and rearranged into countries based only on a few individuals in each country), reveal a rich-list which include: eight individuals from South Africa (24.7), three from Nigeria (19.04), and an individual each from Angola (2.8), Tanzania (1.5), and Kenya (1.0).

Factors contributing to Africa's huge debt profile include the following: The use of foreign aid as a sweetener for disadvantageous trade deals (e.g., EU-Africa trade and development ties in relation to free-market opening under Economic Partnership Agreements, or EPAs). The securitisation of development which allows for foreign political influence and military presence in the continent (e.g., the current military presence of the US and France in the Sahel in the various forms of military bases and armed intervention forces). The use of foreign aid as an inducement to influence local policies through "policy dialogue" between donor and recipient nations. The use of threat and application of sanctions against nations who object or fail to comply with regulations imposed by foreign corporations or agencies. And irresponsible foreign corporate behaviours that undermine local economies due to abusive exploitation of her resources (e.g., the current exploitation of war-torn Democratic Republic of Congo, thrown into internal conflicts while a foreign corporation mines her mineral. resources). Another factor responsible for Africa's huge debt burden is unfair foreign trade. Interestingly, the colonial economic structures set up to export raw materials, and import manufactures remain in place in most of the continent. Tariffs are, for instance, set low for African raw materials and high for manufactures, making it easier to export raw materials than to manufacture. However, while agricultural raw materials (e.g., cocoa, coffee, tobacco, cotton, oil palm) are uplifted from Africa at very low prices, they are returned in their finished or final states, in various processed forms, at very expensive rates. A perfect single example here is coffee: in 2014, Africa, a major coffee producer, earned only £1.5 billion from the crop while Germany, a leading processor, earned nearly double that amount from coffee re-exports. The main reason for this is that Africa is levied with a 7.5 percent tariff charge on roasted coffee by the EU but none for non-decaffeinated green coffee. Consequently, the bulk of her export to the EU is unroasted green coffee, at a great advantage to German coffee-processing companies. EU tariff charge on processed cocoa is as high as 30 percent. On the other hand, policies in Europe, such as the Common Agricultural Policy (CAP), through which huge subsidies are made available to

major EU farmers, make manufactures significantly cheaper in
Europe than in Africa. As a result, manufactures from the continent struggle in their export market, as well as locally, having
been underpriced in local markets by cheaper European imports.
It is estimated that Africa currently imports about 80 percent of
her food.

There is also the "Structural Adjustment Programs"
(SAPs) foisted on Africa during the 1980s and 1990s—in
response to the African economic crisis of the 1970s—as a result
of which little industrial capabilities most countries mastered
following colonisation either completely died off, or became
greatly diminished, in addition to leaving participating countries
heavily indebted and with huge foreign debt portfolios. The
program consisted of loans provided by the International
Monetary Fund (IMF) and the World Bank (WB) to countries in
Africa believed to be undergoing economic crises. Both
institutions required Debtor-nations to implement certain
policies before they could obtain new loans or in order to lower
interest rates on existing loans. Such policies include, but not
exclusively: currency devaluation (to achieve a reduction in
Balance of Payment deficits), austerity measures (including
higher taxes and lower government spending in order to reduce
budget deficit), restructuring foreign debts, eliminating food
subsidies, privatisation or divestiture of all or part of state-owned
enterprises, enhancing the rights of foreign investors, and
focusing economic output on direct export and resource
extraction most of which left a detrimental impact on Africa's
agricultural sector. Needless to point out that SAPs have been
more damaging, in so many ways, than beneficial to the African
(and other) countries who took part in the program as loan

recipients. Furthermore, the Economic Partnership Agreements (EPAs) trade and development agreements negotiated between the EU and countries from Africa, the Caribbean, and the Pacific (ACP) engaged in regional economic integration processes, which came into force in June 2000 following the "Cotonou Agreement" between the ACP and EU, only allow for the continued exploitation of the continent by big European businesses as they seem more designed to open up the markets of African countries for EU exports. While the EPAs requires both sides to lower tariffs on imports and exports, the actual terms are not collectively agreed upon. Instead, some room is left for specific terms to be arranged independently between European partners and African countries on an individual basis. Both reduce the bargaining power of each African country while also rendering them vulnerable to exploitative manipulation through one corrupt practice or another (e.g., the promise from EU partners of spurious foreign aid or personal assets in exchange for unbalanced trade deals in favour of Europe and to Africa's disadvantage). These strategies ensure Africa is never debt-free.

Another aspect of the curses in Deuteronomy related to racism is this: ***The heaven which is over your head shall be bronze, and the earth which is under you, iron.*** *The LORD will make the rain of your land powder and dust; from heaven it will come down on you until you are destroyed. The LORD will cause you to be defeated before your enemies; you will go out against them one way, but flee before them seven ways, and you will be an example of terror to all the kingdoms of the earth [when they see your destruction].* ***Your carcasses will be food for all the birds of the sky and the beasts of the earth,*** *and there will be no one to frighten*

them away (Deuteronomy 28: 23–26 AMP). Although the reference to bronze heaven and iron earth is figurative,
indicative of the absence of rainfall and of land which is difficult to cultivate, this was also literally the case during transatlantic slavery where some enslaved African blacks were secured in metal cages during auctions or while being transported to prevent them from escaping—in these cages, the "heaven over their head" was "bronze" (metal) while the "earth under them" was iron (metal). Even though slavery is now abolished, this remains the case as represented in the disproportionate imprisonment of blacks in the US and parts of Europe. The Thirteenth Amendment to the US Constitution (Amendment XIII) abolished slavery and involuntary servitude, except as punishment for a crime, but exempts penal labour from its prohibition of forced labour, thus requiring convicted prisoners to engage in involuntary labour or face other punishment while in custody. The American Civil Liberties Union (ACLU) sources show that although the US population is about 5 percent of the world's population, the country had nearly 25 percent of the world's prison population. The country's prison population has also increased since 1970 by 700 percent, far outpacing population growth and crime rate. Records of the US Bureau of Justice Statistics (BJS) show that 2,220,300 adults were incarcerated in US federal and state prisons and county jails in 2013; about 0.91 percent of adults (1 in 110) in the US resident population. But then, the disparity in the racial composition of the prison population in the US is such that "one out of every three black boys born today can expect to go to prison in his lifetime compared to one out of every seventeen white boys," according to ACLU sources. A CNN source reported that "African-Americans continue to make up a disproportionate

amount of the prison population," further stating that the racial imbalance of the prison population in the USA "has been a defining characteristic of the criminal justice system for years, and it is still the case today." Significantly, "though African-Americans comprise only about 12% of the total US population, they represent 33 percent of the federal and state prison population," according to a CNN source. Mass incarceration in the USA and the associated racial imbalance of the prison population in the country is the main subject of civil rights advocate and legal scholar Michelle Alexander's book, *The New Jim Crow: Mass Incarceration in the Age of Colorblindness* (2010). In this book, she argues that contrary to the conventional point of view that racial discrimination has mostly ended in the USA with the civil rights reforms of the 1960s, the country's criminal justice system uses the war on drugs as a primary tool for enforcing traditional, as well as new modes of racial discrimination and repression. These new modes of racism, in her opinion, are responsible for the country's incarceration rate being the highest in the world and also the disproportionate incarceration of African-American men. The fact that the incarceration and crime-commission rates are not evenly matched when broken down into racial categories—whites are more likely to commit drug crimes in the US than non-whites—led Alexander to conclude that "the primary targets of the control can be defined largely by race" and that mass incarceration is "a stunningly comprehensive and well-disguised system of racialized social control that functions in a manner strikingly similar to Jim Crow." Furthermore, a report submitted to the United Nations (UN) by The Sentencing Project includes the following statistics: At the end of 2015, black adults are 5.9 times as likely to be incarcerated than white adults. As of 2001, one of every three black boys born in that year could expect to go to prison in his lifetime compared to one of every seventeen white boys. In 2016, blacks comprised 27% of all individuals arrested in the USA, representing twice their share of the total population. Black youths accounted for 15% of all children in the USA yet made up 35% of juvenile arrests in 2016, more than one in four people arrested for drug law violations in 2015 was black, and blacks were 3.7 times more likely to be arrested for marijuana possession than whites in 2010. In recent years, black drivers have been somewhat more likely to be stopped than whites but have been far more likely to be searched and arrested, blacks were incarcerated in local jails at a rate 3.5 times higher than that of whites in 2016, and 48% of the 206,000 people serving life and "virtual life" prison sentences are blacks.

A similar situation obtains in the UK where 2017 national statistics from the Ministry of Justice show that in 2016 to 2017, stops and searches by the Police Force were eight times more likely to target blacks than whites while arrests were three and a half times more likely to target blacks relative to their population size. Relative to population also, the rates of prosecution for indictable offences were four times higher for blacks than whites. In 2016, black defendants were 23% more likely than white defendants to be remanded in custody in Crown Court for indictable offences; blacks have consistently had the highest average custodial sentence length (ACSL) since 2012. The prosecution rate relative to the population was highest for black juveniles (12 juveniles per 1,000 people in the population compared to 2 juveniles per 1,000 for whites); the prison population show that there were 58 black prisoners for every 10,000 people compared to 16 white prisoners for every 10,000 people.

In most prisons, inmates are "caged" in ways similar to the slavery cages, figuratively. Similarly, the reference to their carcasses being meat to the birds and land beasts resonates with what occurred in the US during and shortly after slavery with the lynching of African Americans whose corpses were often left hanging on trees unattended and free for birds and beasts to feast upon.

Identity Fraud

The misappropriation of the identity, heritage, and achievement of black people through the process of "whitewashing" is yet another significant aspect of Jacob's Trouble. The term "whitewash" was originally used to imply a cover-up (e.g., of an unpleasant fact to keep it hidden) or of an undesirable condition of a building by giving it a quick paint-over with a fresh coat of white paint (aptly named "whitewash"). However, the term would later also be used metaphorically, in a social and racial context, to collectively describe various conducts and practices through which a white identity is tactfully superimposed over a black one in an attempt to minimise the latter. The aspect of Jacob's Trouble related to whitewashing is perhaps the most troubling and damaging because it ensures the people so affected remain perpetual victims. The only way out of the trouble is by the affected people turning from the very things which necessitated the curses in the first place—disobedience to God, thus breaching the covenant between God and Abraham. To do this, the people must first be aware of who they truly are, Abraham's descendants, and why they are "troubled." Otherwise, the risk remains of them operating under the consequences of the curses from generation to generation unending, which seems to have been the case until now.

Since the "get-out-of-jail card" is hidden in their real identity, the restoration of these modern-day descendants of ancient Israelites hinges greatly on them rediscovering their true identity and heritage, first and foremost. Therefore, anything which makes it difficult for them to rediscover their true identity represents the biggest obstacle against their restoration. This is exactly what whitewashing in this context represents.

Although history is generally whitewashed, having been written by European historians and presented in their favour, the history of Israel is particularly whitewashed so much so that her true geography and the true identity of her people is not only hidden but has also been grossly misappropriated and misrepresented. The true location of ancient Israel, for instance, is the subject of many scholarly debates, including the full extent of her boundaries. Fortunately, the information in this regard is provided in the Hebrew Bible as already noted. Regarding identity, the true Israelites are commonly regarded as "lost," as though they somehow became extinct, while the term "Jew" became widely preferred as a subtle but dubious alternative to "Israelites." Consequently, instead of "Israelites" or "Hebrews", as they were referred to in older secular and scriptural records, "Jew" became the term of choice in both secular and scriptural records in later historical periods; interestingly, only after the people were conquered and expelled from their land. This substitution may seem reasonable and harmless but, upon closer scrutiny, could be deliberate and part of a plan. A very elaborate and ominous plan. For instance, it has made it easy for most people who are Jewish by religion to claim Israel as their nationality and also to be widely accepted as such. This then makes it very difficult to know who is an Israelite by ancestry, or to separate the latter from those who claim to be Israelites but only by religion. Furthermore, since the popular Israelites in modern history are those who claim to be so as a result of their religion (Jews), it is even harder for the true ancestral Israelites to realise who they truly are, especially because modern history refers to the former group as Israelites. Having been taught accordingly, from birth, how could anyone believe otherwise? The result is what obtains today, with the true ancestral Israelites believing the Jews to be the historical Israelites while remaining innocently ignorant that they are indeed the real Israelites. Except for supernatural intervention, it is almost impossible for this ignorance to be broken.

Fortunately, this has proven to be the case recently as more Black Africans in different parts of the world are gradually dawning on the realisation of who the true Israelites are, although such realisation is not always totally accurate in some cases. For instance, there are some who now believe that all Black Africans are descended from ancient Israelites, while others believe that only African Americans are the true Israelites. The truth, however, is that the true Israelites are hidden within the current global black population, including in and outside Africa, where they have become assimilated over many centuries. With time though, I believe, everyone with an Israelite ancestry would be awakened to that reality through a supernatural process—as it was in my case.

Next to identity in whitewashing is heritage. In this regard, the most whitewashed is the true spiritual heritage of Israelites. The real people whose history is the main subject of the Hebrew Bible are not aware the stories relate to them but instead, many believe the stories are about a lost people who somehow have subsequently reemerged as the Jews who are now represented as Israelites, howbeit inaccurately. This has been enabled by the rewriting of history, which presents an incomplete and inaccurate narrative of the events being reported.

The African origin of humans, for instance, in uncommon knowledge while the history of Africa before transatlantic slavery and colonisation is also relatively unknown. Incidentally, a complete and accurate history of Africa up to transatlantic slavery would reveal the presence of the ancient Israelites in the region, including when and how they got there. Likewise, a complete and accurate rendition of Africa's history during transatlantic slavery would reveal how these ancient Israelites, then in Africa, were specifically targeted for enslavement resulting in their being scattered across other parts of the world, particularly the Americas and Europe. Instead, this aspect of Africa's history remains hidden while a different narrative is invented and popularised, one which is both incomplete and inaccurate. Research conducted by the Teaching Tolerance project of the Southern Poverty Law Center (SPLC), a human rights campaign and activist group in the US, reveal that in the country, "Schools are not adequately teaching the history of American slavery. Educators are not sufficiently prepared to

teach it. Textbooks do not have enough material about it."
Teaching Tolerance conducted online surveys in 2017 of 1,000
US high-school seniors and more than 1,700 social-studies
teachers across the country; and also reviewed 10 commonly used
US-history textbooks, and examined 15 sets of state standards to
assess what students knew, what educators taught, what
publishers included, and what existing standards required with
respect to slavery. The results were staggering and included the
following: While 92 percent of the teachers surveyed claimed
they were "comfortable discussing slavery" in their classrooms,
and additional results showed that only 52 percent taught their
students about slavery's legal roots in the country's founding
documents, only 53 percent emphasised the extent of slavery
outside of the antebellum South (before the US Civil War), and
just 54 percent taught the continuing legacy of slavery in today's
society somehow belied their original claim while also
representing profound lapses in their teaching practices.
Additionally, a high proportion of teachers relied on simulations,
involving role-playing and games, to teach slavery, which could
easily lead to oversimplification and stereotypes, while a
significant majority (73 percent) made use of "slaves" instead of
"enslaved persons" when talking about slavery in the classroom.
The latter is preferable because it emphasises the humanity of the
victims of slavery. It is noteworthy that an overwhelming
majority of teachers who took part in the survey (90 percent) are
somehow affiliated with Teaching Tolerance and its learning
materials; which Maureen Costello, the director of Teaching
Tolerance, said indicated the problems revealed in the survey
results could be much more pervasive than the findings suggested
because the collection of survey respondents represented "a

group more sensitive to issues of race, more likely to confront them in classrooms" compared to the broader teacher workforce, while also adding that the findings are "a silhouette of the problem." Furthermore, many of those surveyed were elementary-school teachers, which Costello said was equally noteworthy considering the ability of slavery education in the early grades to form the narrative, the "fake history," which students carry through high school. With respect to textbooks and state content standards, Teaching Tolerance found that textbooks generally lacked comprehensive coverage of slavery and enslaved people—the best textbook earned a score of 70 on the project's rating of essential elements for bringing slavery into the classroom, notable among which are: Enslaved and free people of African descent had a profound impact on American culture, producing leaders and literary, artistic and folk traditions that continue to influence the nation. Slavery shaped the fundamental beliefs of Americans about race and whiteness, and white supremacy was both a product and legacy of slavery. Enslaved people resisted the efforts of their enslavers to reduce them to commodities in both revolutionary and everyday ways. Protections for slavery were embedded in the founding documents, enslavers dominated the federal government, Supreme Court and Senate from 1787 through 1860. Slavery and the slave trade were central to the development and growth of the economy across British North America and, later, the United States; and Slavery, which was practiced by Europeans prior to their arrival in the Americas, was important to all of the colonial powers and existed in all of the European North American colonies. It also found that state standards were generally "timid," focusing more on abolitionists than on the everyday experience of slavery. For the students surveyed, the project's findings included the following: Among 12th-graders, only 8 percent could identify slavery as the cause of the Civil War, fewer than one-third (32 percent) correctly named the 13th Amendment as the formal end of slavery in the United States, with 35 percent wrongly choosing the Emancipation Proclamation, fewer than half (46 percent) identified the "Middle Passage" as the transport of enslaved Africans across the Atlantic Ocean to North America; fewer than one-quarter (22 percent) of participating high-school seniors knew that "protections for slavery were embedded in America's founding documents," that rather than a "peculiar institution" of the South, slavery was a Constitutionally enshrined right; and fewer than four in ten students surveyed (39 percent) understood how slavery "shaped the fundamental beliefs of Americans about race and whiteness."

In the UK, it was only as recently as in 2008 that authorities in Britain, whose involvement and role in the transatlantic slavery was very significant, decided to make slavery history lessons compulsory for all secondary pupils in England, starting from September that year, despite the fact that the slave trade is an integral part of British history. The key components of the proposed curricula, however, raise questions as to how complete, accurate, and effective these lessons would be, or if they will at all be any different from how similar lessons are taught in the US as noted. Featuring William Wilberforce and Olaudah Equiano as a key component of the proposed curricula, for instance, suggests an overemphasis on abolitionism, as in the US.

Religion is another tool that has been used in

whitewashing in this context: Some of the world's major religions particularly, Judaism, Christianity, and Islam, have been modified to align with particular narratives and to suit particular agenda, most of which deny the true Israelites their true spiritual heritage. In Judaism, the Jews are presented as the "Chosen Ones," while in Christianity, Christians are regarded as the "Spiritual Israelites," in a case of subtle replacement in both cases. Islam, on the other hand, rejects Isaac as the "Promised Child" while presenting Ishmael as the rightful heir to Abraham and his legacy. A serious implication here is that subscribing to any of these religions—which happen to be the more popular among the modern black population—would make it almost impossible for the true Israelites realising their true heritage and the future awaiting them, which they ought to be expecting and be preparing for, thus contributing towards their existing ignorance as well as the deception sustained by it but more importantly, in perpetuating Jacob's Trouble.

Illustrations

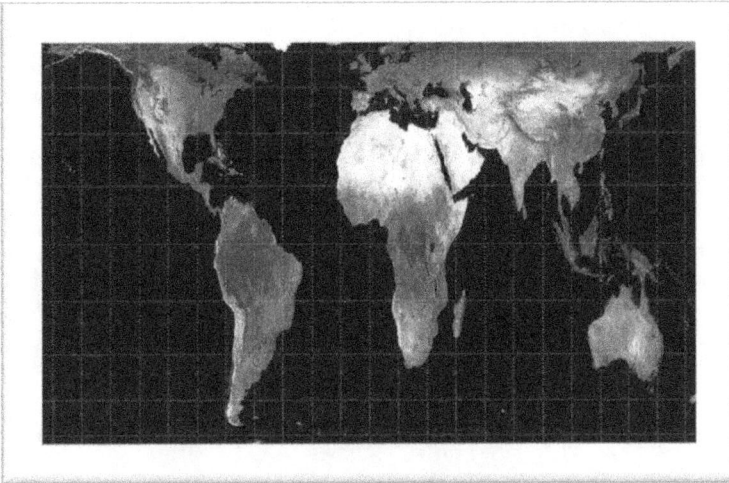

Fig 1a. World map based on Gall-Peter's projection showing a more accurate size of Africa. Source:https://commons.wikimedia.org/wiki/File:Arno_Peters-Projektion.JPG .

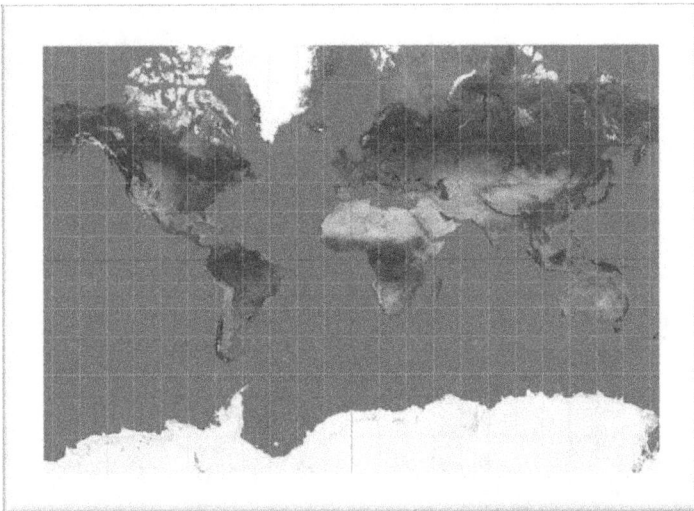

Fig 1b. World map based on Mercator's projection showing Africa smaller. Credit: Daniel R.Strebe

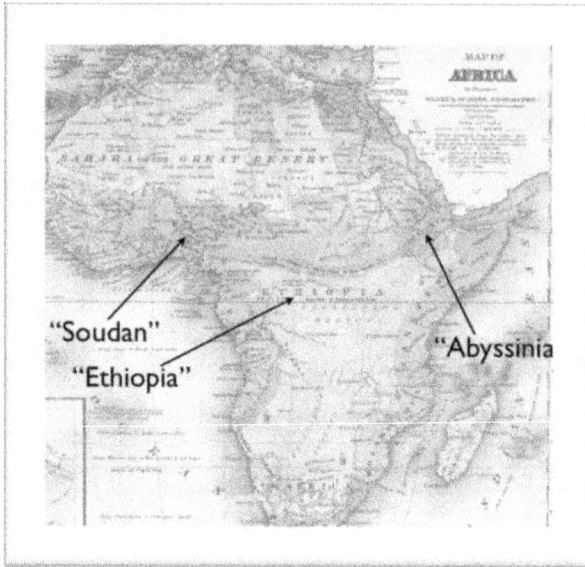

Fig 2a. Ancient map of Africa showing the region known as Ethiopia.
Source: Martin W. Lewis,

Fig 2b. Ancient map of West Africa showing a Kingdom of Judah.
Credit: Bowen, E. (1747)

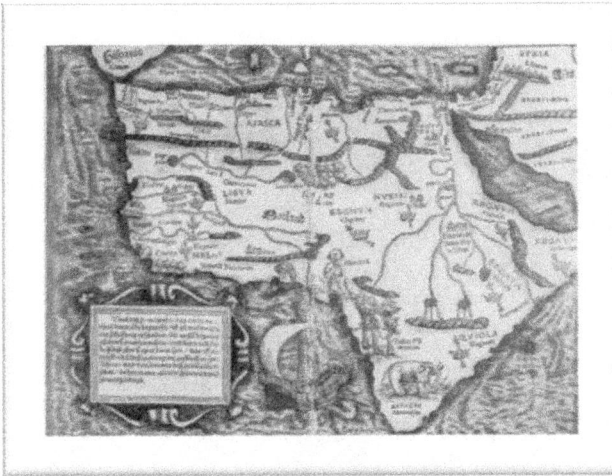

Fig 3a. Ancient map of Africa showing part of today's Middle East as part of Africa's tectonic plate. Credit: Vladislav Gurfinkel

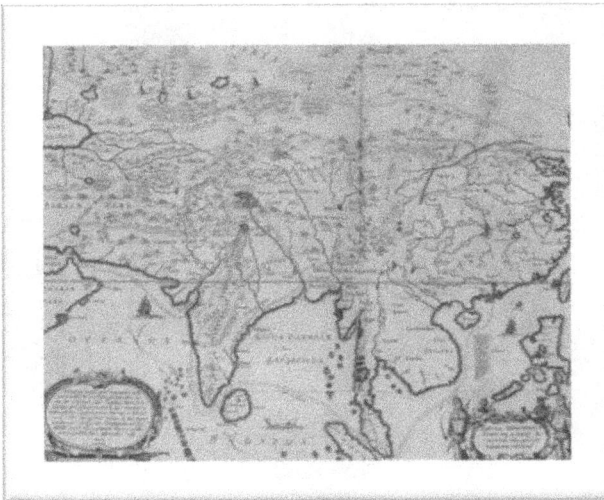

Fig 3b. A historical map of old Eurasia (1670). Source: https://www.mapsof.net/asia/historical-map-of-asia-1670

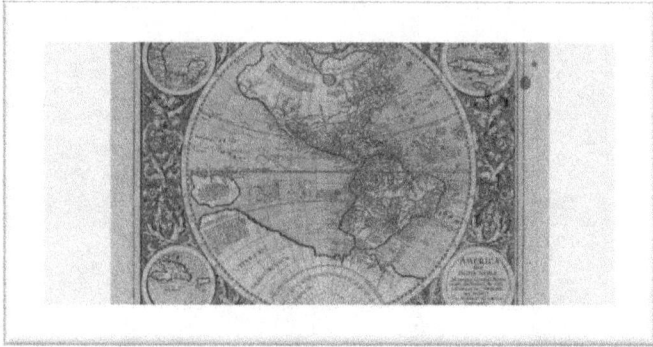

Fig 3c. A historical map of the old Americas. Credit: The New York Public Library

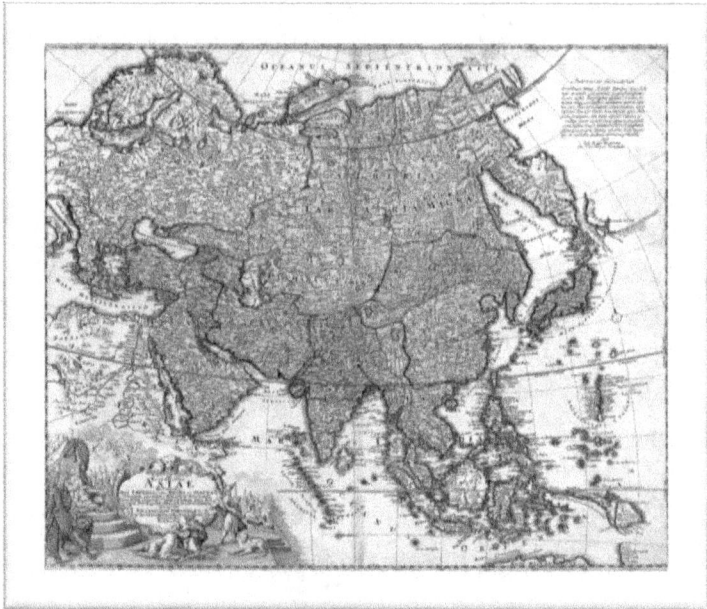

Fig 3d. A historical map of old Eurasia and Australasia (1743).

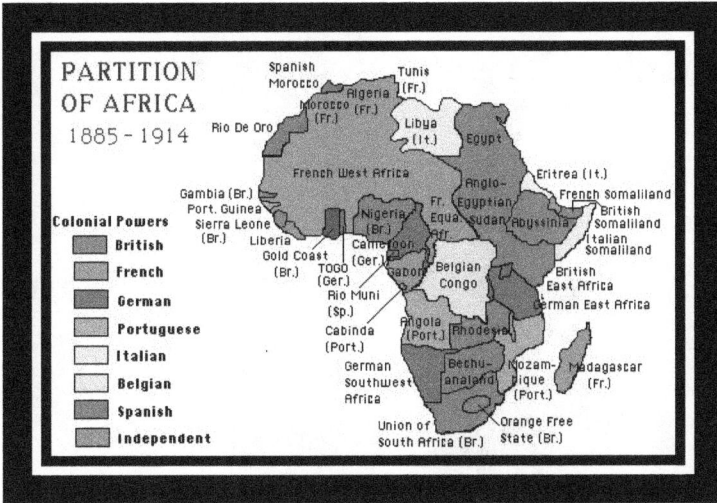

Fig 4a. The Partition of Africa during colonisation. Credit: y Ro Ho

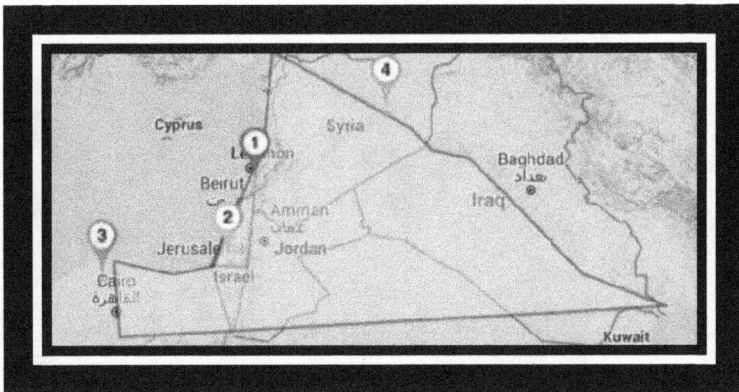

Fig 4b. Map showing the biblical boundaries of Israel.

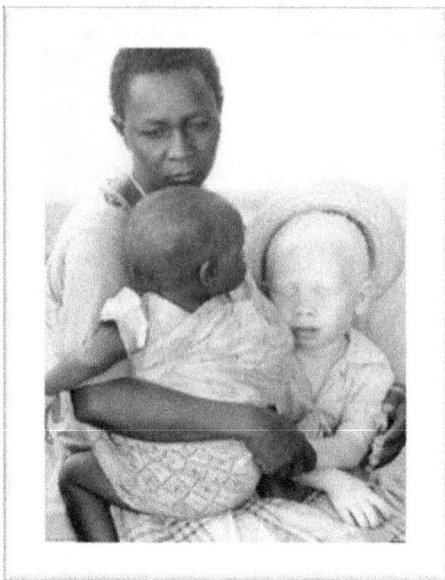

Fig 5a. Albinism.
Source: BBC.

Fig 5b. Albinism: Black mother with white children.
Source: The Mirror.

Fig 5c. Albinism. Black parents with a white child.
Source: New York Post

Fig 6a. Black American-Indians.

Fig 6b. Black Europe: Black people in renaissance Europe.
Source: New York Times

Fig 6c. Black Europe: Moorish kings and queens in Europe

Fig 7a. An Oba of ancient Benin Kingdom.
Credit: Giulio Ferrario

Fig 8a. Captives on board a slave ship on the coast of West Africa c.1880..
Credit: Ann Ronan Pictures/ Getty Images)

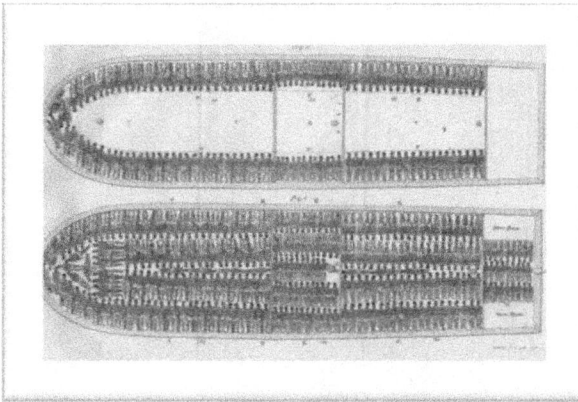

Fig 8b. Diagram of the "Brookes" slave ship. By Thomas Clarkson. Source:
The Britsh Library.

In Honor of Black History Month
BLACK INVENTORS

PRODUCT	INVENTOR	DATE
Air Conditioning Unit	Frederick M. Jones	1949
Almanac	Benjamin Banneker	1791
Auto Cut-Off Switch	Granville T. Woods	1839
Auto Fishing Device	George Cook	1899
Baby Buggy	William H. Richardson	1889
Biscuit Cutter	Alexander P. Ashbourne	1875
Blood Plasma Bag	Charles Drew	1945
Chamber Commode	Thomas Elkins	1897
Clothes Dryer	George T. Sampson	1971
Curtain Rod	Samuel R. Scrottron	1892
Curtain Rod Support	William S. Grant	1896
Door Knob	Osbourn Dorsey	1878
Door Stop	Osbourn Dorsey	1878
Egg Beater	Willie Johnson	1884
Electric Lamb Bulb	Lewis Latimer	1882
Elevator	Alexander Miles	1867
Eye Protector	Powell Johnson	1880
Fire Escape Ladder	Joseph W. Winters	1878
Fire Extinguisher	Thomas Marshall	1872
Folding Bed	Leonard C. Bailey	1899
Folding Chair	Nathaniel Alexander	1911
Fountain Pen	Walter B. Purvis	1890
Furniture Caster	David A. Fisher	1878
Gas Mask	Garrett Morgan	1914
Golf Tee	George T. Grant	1899
Guitar	Robert F. Fleming, Jr.	1886
Hair Brush	Lydia O. Newman	1898
Hand Stamp	Walter B. Purvis	1883
Ice Cream Scoop	Alfred L. Cralle	1897
Insect Destroyer Gun	Albert C. Richardson	1899
Ironing Board	Sarah Boone	1887
Key Chain	Frederick J. Loudin	1894
Lantern	Michael C. Harvey	1884
Lawn Sprinkler	John H. Smith	1897
Lemon Squeezer	John Thomas White	1893
Lock	Washington A. Martin	1893
Lubricating Cup	Elijah McCoy	1895
Lunch Pail	James Robinson	1887
Mail Box	Paul L. Downing	1891
Mop	Thomas W. Stewart	1893
Peanut Butter	George W. Carver	1896
Pencil Sharpener	John L. Love	1897
Record Player Arm	Joseph H. Dickinson	1819
Rolling Pin	John W. Reed	1864
Shampoo Headrest	Charles Orren Bailiff	1898
Spark Plug	Edmond Berger	1839
Stethoscope	Thomas A. Carrington	1876
Straightening Comb	Madam C. J. Walker	1905
Street Sweeper	Charles B. Brooks	1890
Phone Transmitter	Granville T. Woods	1884
Thermostat Control	Frederick M. Jones	1960
Traffic Light	Garrett Morgan	1923
Tricycle	Matthew A. Cherry	1886

Fig 9. A list of Black inventors and inventions.
Credit: Natasha Abdullah.

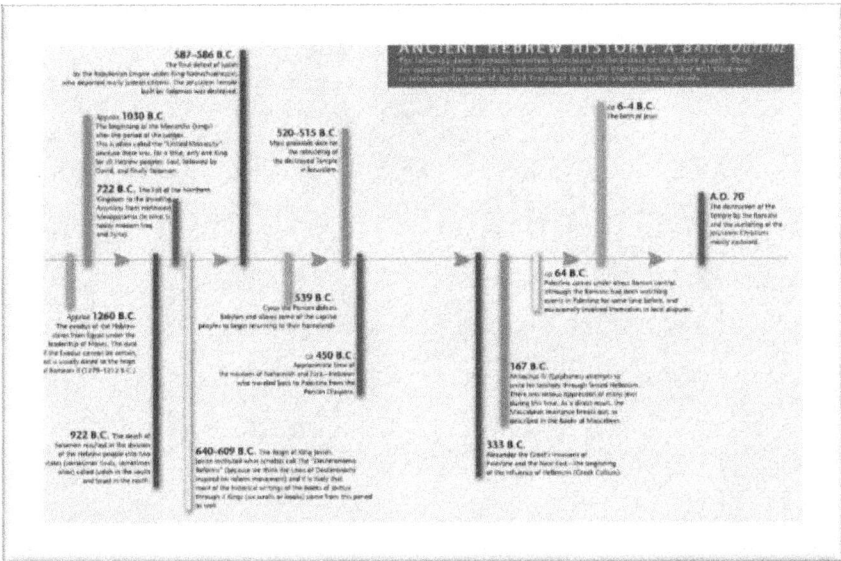

Fig 10. Timeline of biblical history of Israel up to AD 70.
Credit: Bing Imag

CHAPTER SIX

The Promise

The curses—Jacob's Trouble—are not meant to be everlasting, nor are they without a remedy. There is an expiry time, and there is what is needed to turnaround the predicament, all of which are detailed in different prophecies in the Hebrew Bible. The most common and most direct of these prophecies are those given by the prophet Isaiah, including the following: ***And there shall come forth a shoot out of the stock of Jesse, and a branch out of his roots shall be fruitful; and the Spirit of Jehovah shall rest upon him, the spirit of wisdom and understanding, the spirit of counsel and might, the spirit of knowledge and of the fear of Jehovah.*** *And his delight will be in the fear of Jehovah; and he shall not judge after the sight of his eyes, neither reprove after the hearing of his ears; but with righteousness shall he judge the poor, and reprove with equity the meek of the earth: and he shall smite the earth with the rod of his mouth, and with the breath of his lips shall he slay the wicked. And righteousness shall be the girdle of his reins, and* *faithfulness the girdle of his loins. The wolf also shall dwell with the lamb, and the leopard shall lie down with the kid, and the calf and the young lion and the fatted beast together, and a little child shall lead them. And the cow and the she-bear shall feed; their young ones shall lie down together; and the lion shall eat straw like the ox. And the sucking child shall play on the hole of the adder, and the weaned child shall put forth its hand to the viper's den. They shall not hurt nor destroy in all my holy mountain; for the earth shall be full of the knowledge of Jehovah, as the waters cover the sea. And in that day there shall be a root of Jesse, standing as a banner of the peoples: the nations shall seek it; and his resting-place shall be glory.* **And it shall come to pass in that day, that the Lord shall set his hand again the second time to acquire the remnant of his people which shall be left, from Assyria, and from Egypt, and from Pathros, and from Cush, and from Elam, and from Shinar, and from Hamath, and from the islands of the sea. And he shall lift up a banner to the nations, and shall assemble the outcasts of Israel, and gather together the dispersed of Judah from the four corners of the earth.** *And the envy of Ephraim shall depart, and the troublers of Judah shall be cut off; Ephraim will not envy Judah, and Judah will not trouble Ephraim: but they shall fly upon the shoulder of the Philistines towards the west; together shall they spoil the sons of the east; they shall lay their hand upon Edom and Moab, and the children of Ammon shall obey them* (Isaiah 11: 1–14 DARBY). And also this: *For Jehovah will have mercy on Jacob, and will yet choose Israel, and set them in rest in their own land; and the stranger shall be united to them, and they shall be joined to the house of Jacob. And the peoples shall take them and bring them to their place; and the house of Israel shall possess them in the land of*

Jehovah for servants and handmaids; **and they shall take them** **captive whose captives they were, and they shall rule over their op-** **pressors.** *And it shall come to pass in the day that Jehovah shall give thee rest from thy sorrow and from thy trouble and from the hard bondage wherein thou wast made to serve* (Isaiah 14: 1–3 DARBY).

The first thing to note, and very crucial too, is that common interpretations and commentaries of biblical texts are heavily influenced by various theologies associated with Christianity, most of which are based on extra-contextual understanding and interpretation. In Christianity, biblical texts are often interpreted out of context for the purpose of supporting a theology or doctrine, thus rendering such texts abused, misunderstood, and unfit for their original purpose. In this regard, the first five verses of Isaiah 11—as referenced—is a good instance. The character who is the subject of these verses, described as a shoot out of the stock of Jesse, is presented in Christianity as Jesus Christ. However, the records presented for Jesus Christ do not match some key defining characteristics given for the subject.

Firstly, it is unclear how Jesus Christ is descended from the stock of Jesse, who is the father of David, the second king of Israel. The first chapter of Matthew in the New Testament Bible gives a genealogy of Jesus, which presents him as "the son of David, the son of Abraham" while also noting that his conception was "of the Holy Ghost." Since a person's lineage is traced paternally, if Jesus Christ was not conceived by the seed of a man, it is then illogical and inaccurate describing him as a son of David even if Mary, the woman he was born by, was a descendant of

David. There is a further contradiction presented in the sixteenth verse when the lineage being traced from Abraham is suddenly connected to "Joseph the husband of Mary, of whom was born Jesus, who is called Christ." This is in clear contradiction of the claim in verse twenty that Jesus was conceived of the Holy Ghost. The account given in Luke 3 of the genealogy of Jesus presented a different lineage which traces Joseph the husband of Mary, of whom Jesus was not conceived by, to David, and Abraham. This raises the very serious question of how a child's ancestry can rightly be traced to a man who is not his biological father.

Secondly, verse two of Isaiah 11 described the subject as someone upon whom the spirit of the Lord shall rest while subsequently listing six specified aspects of the spirit of the Lord that will rest upon him. A contradiction arises when Jesus, who supposedly is the Lord himself (God), is presented as the subject matter here because it becomes unclear how and why the spirit of the Lord would rest upon "the Lord" when the Lord naturally ought to already possess his spirit—the spirit of the Lord.

Thirdly, Isaiah 11: 3–5 goes further to describe a judicial function of the subject matter none which Jesus performed, based on the available records related to him. Note that if this particular function is yet to be fulfilled perhaps in the alleged second coming of Jesus Christ, then, it means that the prophecy in verses eleven and twelve are also yet to be fulfilled because it did say in verse eleven, and it shall come to pass in that day. Furthermore, verses six to ten further describe a scenario that can only be futuristic since none of the events described has ever happened yet.

What the foregoing imply is that Jesus is not the subject matter in this prophecy, and the event described in the eleventh and twelfth verses are futuristic and so have not yet been fulfilled.

The event in question represents the true restoration of Israel, while the Isaiah 11 prophecy represents the promise. As previously noted, a careful analysis of this prophecy would reveal the places from where the remnant of Israel would be drawn, and also that after this restoration, Israel will never again go into captivity. The other reference, Isaiah 14: 1–3, also speaks of this restoration but has similarly been misinterpreted based on wrong Christian theology, with the suggestion that it has already been fulfilled. This is, however, untrue and is evidenced in this phrase in the prophecy: *and they shall take them captive whose captives they were, and they shall rule over their oppressors.* From their very first conquest and expulsion—of the northern kingdom by Assyrians—till date, Israel has never taken captives of any people to whom they were once captives, nor have they ruled over any of their oppressors from Egyptians, Assyrians, Babylonians, Medes and Persians, Greeks, Romans, or their various contemporary counterparts in successive historical periods. This again strongly implies that the promised restoration of Israel is yet to be fulfilled, which among others, reveal the true nature of the present nation of Israel and her people.

The Promised Land

It was noted that the ancient Israelites never really fully inhabited the whole land promised them before their conquest and expulsion began, starting with the defeat of the northern kingdom by the Assyrians starting from c. 740 BC. Numbers 34: 1–15 gives a comprehensive description of the borders of the land

as promised to Abraham by God. (see fig 4b) The land apportioned to nine and a half tribes of Israel is detailed thus: *And
Jehovah spoke to Moses, saying, Command the children of Israel,
and say unto them, When ye come into the land of Canaan, this
shall be the land that shall fall to you for an inheritance, the land
of Canaan according to the borders thereof. Then your south side
shall be from the wilderness of Zin alongside of Edom, and your
southern border shall be from the end of the salt sea eastward;
and your border shall turn from the south of the ascent of
Akrabbim, and pass on to Zin, and shall end southward at
Kadesh-barnea, and shall go on to Hazar-Addar, and pass on to
Azmon. And the border shall turn from Azmon unto the torrent
of Egypt, and shall end at the sea. And as west border ye shall
have the great sea, and its coast. This shall be your west border.
And this shall be your north border: from the great sea ye shall
mark out for you mount Hor; from mount Hor ye shall mark out
the entrance to Hamath, and the end of the border shall be toward
Zedad; and the border shall go to Ziphron, and shall end at
Hazar-enan. This shall be your north border. And ye shall mark
out for you as eastern border from Hazar-enan to Shepham: and
the border shall go down from Shepham to Riblah, on the east
side of Ain; and the border shall descend, and shall strike upon
the extremity of the sea of Chinnereth eastward; and the border
shall go down to the Jordan, and shall end at the salt sea. This
shall be your land according to the borders thereof round about.
And Moses commanded the children of Israel, saying, This is the
land which ye shall take for yourselves as inheritance by lot,
which Jehovah commanded to give to the nine tribes, and to the
half tribe. For the tribe of the children of the Reubenites*

according to their fathers' houses, and the tribe of the children of the Gadites according to their fathers' houses, have received, and half the tribe of Manasseh have received their inheritance; the two tribes and the half tribe have received their inheritance on this side the Jordan of Jericho eastward, toward the sun-rising (Numbers 34: 1–15 DARBY). The land inherited by the other two and a half tribes are recorded thus: *And Moses gave a portion to the tribe of the children of Reuben according to their families. And their territory was from Aroer, which is on the bank of the river Arnon, and the city that is in the midst of the ravine, and all the plateau by Medeba; Heshbon, and all her cities that are in the plateau, Dibon, and Bamoth-Baal, and Beth-Baal-meon, And Jah-zah, and Kedemoth, and Mephaath, and Kirjathaim, and*

Sibmah, and Zereth-shahar in the mountain of the vale, and Beth-Peor, and the slopes of Pisgah, and Beth-jeshimoth; all the cities of the plateau, and the whole kingdom of Sihon the king of the Amorites, who reigned at Heshbon, whom Moses smote, him and the princes of Midian, Evi, and Rekem, and Zur, and Hur, and Reba, the chiefs of Sihon dwelling in the land. And Balaam the son of Beor, the diviner, did the children of Israel kill with the sword among them that were slain by them. And the border of the children of Reuben was the Jordan, and its border. This is the inheritance of the children of Reuben according to their families, the cities and their hamlets. And Moses gave a portion to the tribe of Gad, to the children of Gad according to their families. And their territory was Jaazer, and all the cities of Gilead, and half the land of the children of Ammon, to Aroer which is before Rabbah; and from Heshbon to Ramath-Mizpeh, and Betonim; and from Mahanaim to the border of Debir; and in the valley, Beth-haram, and Beth-Nimrah, and Succoth, and Zaphon, the rest of the

kingdom of Sihon the king of Heshbon, the Jordan and its border,
as far as the edge of the sea of Chinnereth beyond the Jordan
eastward. This is the inheritance of the children of Gad according
to their families, the cities and their hamlets. And Moses gave a
portion to half the tribe of Manasseh; and for half the tribe of the
children of Manasseh according to their families: their territory
was from Mahanaim, all Bashan, the whole kingdom of Og the
king of Bashan, and all the villages of Jair, which are in Bashan,
sixty cities. And half Gilead, and Ashtaroth, and Edrei, the cities
of the kingdom of Og in Bashan, belonged to the children of
Machir the son of Manasseh, to the one half of the children of
Machir according to their families. This is that which Moses
allotted for inheritance in the plains of Moab, beyond the Jordan
of Jericho, eastward. But to the tribe of Levi Moses gave no
inheritance: Jehovah the God of Israel is their inheritance, as he
said to them (Joshua 13: 15–33 DARBY).

It has been noted that the Israelites never really got to eventually occupy the full extent of their promised land which they were expected to takeover through military conquest before being subsequently evicted through conquest. The referenced texts nonetheless detail the full stretch of the promised land. Although the Israelites have now been expelled from their land, they will eventually regain them following their restoration. Ezekiel 47–48 elaborates on the boundaries of Israel after her restoration, including how the land is apportioned to the twelve tribes. The extent of the land is recorded thus: *Thus says the Lord GOD, "This shall be the boundary by which you shall divide the land as an inheritance among the twelve tribes of Israel; Joseph shall have two portions. You shall divide it as an inheritance, each one equally with the other. I lifted up My hand and swore to give it to your fathers, and this land shall fall to you as an inheritance. "And this shall be the boundary of the land on the north side: from the Great [Mediterranean] Sea by way of Hethlon to the entrance of Zedad, Hamath, Berothah, Sibraim, which is between the border of Damascus and the border of Hamath; [as far as] Hazer-hatticon, which is on the border of Hauran. So the boundary will extend from the [Mediterranean] Sea to Hazar-enan at the border of Damascus, and on the north, northward, is the border of Hamath. This is the north side. "The east side, from between Hauran, Damascus, Gilead, and the land of Israel, shall be the Jordan; from the north border to the eastern sea you shall measure. This is the east side. "The south side, southward, from Tamar [near the Dead Sea] shall extend as far as the waters of Meribath-kadesh, to the Brook of Egypt and to the Great [Mediterranean] Sea. This is the south side toward the south. "The west side shall be the Great [Mediterranean] Sea, from the south border to a point opposite Lebo-hamath [north of Mount Hermon]. This is the west side. "So you shall divide this land among yourselves according to the tribes of Israel. You shall divide it by lot as an inheritance among yourselves and among the foreigners who stay among you, who give birth to sons among you. They shall be to you as the native-born [in the country] among the children (descendants) of Israel; they shall be allotted an inheritance with you among the tribes of Israel. In whatever tribe the foreigner resides, there shall you give him his inheritance," says the Lord GOD* (Ezekiel 47: 13–23 AMP).

The stipulated boundaries and stretch of land further reveal that the present nation of Israel does not represent the promised restoration because it occupies just a tiny strip of land

in the region formally known as Palestine, and has boundaries
which do not correspond to those contained in the referenced
prophecies. Thus confirming that the promised restoration of
Israel is yet to be fulfilled as prophesied. Note that this promise
to restore Israel will certainly be fulfilled nonetheless because
God keeps every of His promises.

What immediately emerges as one begins to research
Israel (Who and what they are and where they possibly are now),
is that there seems to be a great conspiracy of deception aimed at
ensuring that neither themselves nor anyone else is able to
rediscover them. This deception is so deep that both history and
religion have been deployed as vital weapons of propaganda in
this regard. The questions this raises in my mind include the
following: What is it that so desperately needed to be kept a
secret as to warrant such a degree of propaganda? Of what harm
is it to those who want it to remain a secret? Of what benefit is it
to the people from whom it is kept a secret? How might this secret
impact the world if or when it is revealed? Only time will tell since
time alone holds every secret.

CHAPTER SEVEN

The Restoration

The hope of Israel lies solely in the promise of restoration and in the faithfulness of Him who has promised—the Lord God of their father Abraham (the Hebrew Elohim). The historiography of ancient Israel shows that her peace and prosperity always depended on the obedience of her people to the laws or commandments of the God of their father Abraham, Elohim, particularly as related to the covenant between God and Abraham—the Abrahamic Covenant. Whenever they lived in obedience to God, they were invincible, but whenever they transgressed, they became easy preys to their enemies. And they had many enemies, perhaps because the land allocated to them originally belonged to and was inhabited by other people. Hence, they were to take over and occupy the land through warfare and conquest. Israel first took possession of the land following her victory in the Battle of Jericho, during which the mighty walls of the city came tumbling down after the Israelites complied with the instructions given to them by God through their leader Joshua who succeeded Moses, who had led them in the Exodus from Egypt. The book of Joshua in the Hebrew Bible gives an account of this battle (in chapter 6) and the earlier history of Israel upon taking possession of Canaan, which was later renamed Israel, including what portions of the land was occupied and by what tribes of Israelites. Interestingly, Israel's first victory in the battle against Jericho, a resounding victory, was soon followed by their first-ever defeat in the battle against Ai. The battle against Ai, who had a very small army compared to Israel, is recorded in Joshua 7. The first verse gave the reason for their defeat—the children of Israel trespassed against divine instruction. Ai was later conquered after Israel repented and restituted, followed by several other major victories which culminated in Israel expanding further across the land—details in Joshua 14–17.

From the time Israel first became a nation, this pattern of obedience and disobedience to God, and victory and defeat in battles would become a common trend culminating in the division of the original Kingdom of Israel into a new Northern Kingdom of Israel and a Southern Kingdom of Judah, and the conquest and expulsion of Israelites from their land as already noted. Since the last conquest of Jerusalem, Israel has remained a conquered territory while Israelites have remained "lost in captivity." This unpleasant status quo has been sustained until date by a number of factors, but the greatest of them is ignorance, particularly on the part of the true Israelites of today. Primarily, the people do not know who they truly are. And if they do not, how could they repent and restitute their ways in order to be delivered and restored, as was severally the case with their ancestors? It is noted here that a mistaken identity, or identity crisis, is the biggest obstacle standing in the way of Israel's restoration.

The Path to Restoration

There is a set time and process for the regathering and restoration of Israelites. The timing element, although unknown, is implied in several prophecies related to the restoration of Israel, notably this phrase in Isaiah 11: 11: *And it shall come to pass in that day.* "In that day" denotes a set or appointed time. Long before Israel migrated to Egypt as a people, God had already revealed to Abraham how his descendants, Israel, would sojourn in a foreign for a specified period—four hundred years (Genesis 15: 13). Likewise, regarding the Babylonian conquest and captivity of the Southern Kingdom of Judah, God revealed through Prophet Jeremiah the duration of this captivity—seventy years (Jeremiah 25: 11, see also 2 Chronicles 36: 21 and Daniel 9: 2).

Based on this precedence, it is my reasoned opinion that the later and final restoration of Israel as promised in different prophecies is ordained for an appointed time, even though I am yet to come across any texts specifying the exact time. Perhaps only God knows when.

Regarding the path or process to restoration, a few details are provided in some prophecies by different prophets, notably Joel and Jeremiah. Joel 3 in the Hebrew Bible paints a very graphic picture of the actual restoration: *For behold, in those days, and in that time, when I shall turn again the captivity of Judah and Jerusalem, I will also gather all the nations, and will bring them down into the valley of Jehoshaphat, and I will enter into judgment with them there on account of my people and mine inheritance, Israel,* **whom they have scattered among the nations: and they have parted my land;** *and they have cast lots for my people, and have given a boy for a harlot, and sold a girl for wine, and have drunk it. Yea also, what have ye to do with me, O Tyre and Zidon, and all the districts of Philistia? Will ye render me a recompence? But if ye recompense me, swiftly and speedily will I bring your recompence upon your own head; because ye have taken my silver and my gold, and have carried into your temples my beautiful pleasant things, and the children of Judah and the children of Jerusalem have ye sold unto the children of the Greeks, that ye might remove them far from their border. Behold, I will raise them up out of the place whither ye have sold them, and will bring your recompence upon your own head. And I will sell your sons and your daughters into the hand of the children of Judah, and they shall sell them to the Sabeans, to a nation far off: for Jehovah hath spoken. Proclaim this among the nations: prepare war, arouse the mighty men, let all the men of war draw near, let them come up. Beat your ploughshares into swords, and your pruning-knives into spears; let the weak say, I am strong. Haste ye and come, all ye nations round about, and gather yourselves together. Thither cause thy mighty ones to come down, O Jehovah. Let the nations rouse themselves, and come up to the valley of Jehoshaphat; for there will I sit to judge all the nations round about. Put in the sickle, for the harvest is ripe: come, get you down, for the press is full, the vats overflow; for* *their wickedness is great. Multitudes, multitudes in the valley of decision! For the day of Jehovah is at hand in the valley of decision. The sun and the moon shall be darkened, and the stars shall withdraw their shining. And Jehovah will roar from Zion, and utter his voice from Jerusalem; and the heavens and the earth shall shake: and Jehovah will be a shelter for his people, and the refuge of the children of Israel. And ye shall know that I, Jehovah, am your God dwelling in Zion, my holy mountain; and Jerusalem shall be holy, and no strangers shall pass through her any more. And it shall come to pass in that day, that the mountains shall drop down new wine, and the hills shall flow with milk, and all the water-courses of Judah shall flow with waters; and a fountain shall come forth from the house of Jehovah, and shall water the valley of Shittim. Egypt shall be a desolation, and Edom shall be a desolate wilderness, for the violence against the children of Judah, in that they have shed innocent blood in their land.* **But Judah shall abide for ever, and Jerusalem from generation to generation.** *And I will purge them from the blood from which I had not purged them: for Jehovah dwelleth in Zion* (Joel 3 DARBY).

The highlighted portions of the foregoing text help to show that this prophecy is yet to be fulfilled: Primarily, because Judah is yet to be properly and fully restored as an independent kingdom of ethnic Israelites drawn from around the world, remaining so forever from generation to generation. Otherwise, the entire text is self-explanatory, needing no further commentary. Jeremiah 31 also presents a similar graphic illustration of the actual restoration: *At that time, saith Jehovah, will I be the God of all the families of Israel, and they shall be my people. Thus saith Jehovah: The people that were left of the sword have found grace in the wilderness, even Israel, when I go to give him rest. Jehovah hath appeared from afar unto me, saying, Yea, I have loved thee with an everlasting love; therefore with loving-kindness have I drawn thee. I will build thee again, and thou shalt be built, O virgin of Israel! Thou shalt again be adorned with thy tambours, and shalt go forth in the dances of them that make merry. Thou shalt again plant vineyards upon the mountains of Samaria; the planters shall plant, and shall eat the fruit. For there shall be a day, when the watchmen upon mount Ephraim shall cry, Arise, and let us go up to Zion, unto Jehovah our God For thus saith Jehovah: Sing aloud with gladness for Jacob, and shout at the head of the nations; publish ye, praise ye, and say, Jehovah, save thy people, the remnant of Israel. Behold, I bring them from the north country, and gather them from the uttermost parts of the earth; and among them the blind and the lame, the woman with child and her that travaileth with child together: a great assemblage shall they return hither. They shall come with weeping, and with supplications will I lead them; I will cause them to walk by water-brooks, in a straight way, wherein they shall not stumble; for I will be a father to Israel, and Ephraim is my firstborn. Hear the word of Jehovah, ye nations, and declare it to the isles afar off, and say, He that scattered Israel will gather him, and keep him, as a shepherd his flock. For Jehovah hath ransomed Jacob, and redeemed him from the hand of one stronger than he. And they shall come and sing aloud upon the height of Zion, and shall flow together to the goodness of Jehovah, for corn, and for new wine, and for oil, and for the young of the flock and of the herd; and their soul shall be as a watered garden, and they shall not languish any more at all. Then shall the virgin rejoice in the dance, and the young men and old together; for I will turn their mourning into gladness, and will comfort them, and make them rejoice after their sorrow. And I will satiate the soul of the priests with fatness, and my people shall be satisfied with my goodness, saith Jehovah. Thus saith Jehovah: A voice hath been heard in Ramah, the wail of very bitter weeping, — Rachel weeping for her children, refusing to be comforted for her children, because they are not. Thus saith Jehovah: Refrain thy voice from weeping, and thine eyes from tears; for there is a reward for thy work, saith Jehovah; and they shall come again from the land of the enemy. And there is hope for thy latter end, saith Jehovah, and thy children shall come again to their own border. I have indeed heard Ephraim bemoaning himself thus: Thou hast chastised me, and I was chastised as a bullock not trained: turn thou me, and I shall be turned; for thou art Jehovah my God Surely after that I was turned, I repented; and after I knew myself, I smote upon my thigh. I was ashamed, yea, even confounded, for I bear the reproach of my youth. Is Ephraim a dear son unto me? is he a child of delights? For whilst I have been speaking against him, I do constantly remember him still. Therefore my bowels are troubled for him: I will certainly have mercy upon him, saith Jehovah. Set up waymarks, make for thyself signposts; set thy heart toward the highway, the way by which thou wentest: turn again, O virgin of Israel, turn again to these thy cities. How long wilt thou wander about, thou backsliding daughter? For Jehovah hath created a new thing on the earth, a woman shall encompass a man. Thus saith Jehovah of hosts, the God of Israel: They shall again use this speech, in the land of Judah and in the cities thereof, when I shall turn their captivity: Jehovah bless thee, O habitation of righteousness, mountain of holiness! And therein shall dwell*

Judah, and all the cities thereof together, the husbandmen, and they that go about with flocks. For I have satiated the weary soul, and every languishing soul have I replenished. — Upon this I awaked, and beheld; and my sleep was sweet unto me. Behold, days come, saith Jehovah, that I will sow the house of Israel and the house of Judah with the seed of man and the seed of beast. And it shall come to pass, as I have watched over them, to pluck up, and to break down, and to overthrow, and to destroy, and to afflict; so will I watch over them to build, and to plant, saith Jehovah. In those days they shall say no more, The fathers have eaten sour grapes, and the children's teeth are set on edge: for every one shall die for his own iniquity; every man that eateth the sour grapes, his teeth shall be set on edge. **Behold, days come, saith Jehovah, that I will make a new covenant with the house of Israel and with the house of Judah: not according to the covenant that I made with their fathers, in the day of my taking them by the hand, to lead them out of the land of Egypt; which my covenant they broke, although I was a husband unto them, saith Jehovah. For this is the covenant that I will make with the house of Israel, after those days, saith Jehovah: I will put my law in their inward parts, and will write it in their heart; and I will be their God and they shall be my people. And they shall teach no more every man his neighbour, and every man his brother, saying, Know Jehovah; for they shall all know me, from the least of them unto the greatest of them, saith Jehovah: for I will pardon their iniquity, and their sin will I remember no more.** *Thus saith Jehovah, who giveth the sun for light by day, the ordinances of the moon and of the stars for light by night, who stirreth up the sea so that the waves thereof roar, — Jehovah of hosts is his name: If those ordinances depart from before me, saith Jehovah, the* *seed of Israel also shall cease from being a nation before me for ever. Thus saith Jehovah: If the heavens above can be measured, and the foundations of the earth searched out beneath, I will also cast off the whole seed of Israel, for all that they have done, saith Jehovah. Behold, the days come, saith Jehovah, that the city shall be built to Jehovah, from the tower of Hananeel unto the corner-gate. And the measuring line shall yet go forth before it unto the hill Gareb, and shall turn toward Goath. And the whole valley of the dead bodies, and of the ashes, and all the fields unto the torrent Kidron, unto the corner of the horse-gate toward the east, shall be holy unto Jehovah: it shall not be plucked up, nor overthrown any more for ever* (Jeremiah 31 DARBY).

Again, the referenced text is self-explanatory, needing no further commentary, except for the highlighted portion, which in addition to denoting the futuristic nature of the prophecy, is also useful for the purpose of clarifying another erroneous theology in Christianity. The main subject of the highlighted text is the New Covenant—which Christianity teaches was instituted by Jesus during The Last Supper (Matthew 26: 28, see also Hebrews 12: 24). A careful exegesis of the text in reference, however, shows that the New Covenant is yet to be instituted, as is hereby demonstrated:

Firstly, it was to be made with a united Israel. The prophecy was made at a time when Israel was divided hence the reference to the two houses (kingdoms): *Behold, days come, saith Jehovah, that I will make a new covenant with the house of Israel and with the house of Judah: not according to the covenant that I made with their fathers, in the day of my taking them by the hand, to lead them out of the land of Egypt; which my covenant they broke, although I was a husband unto them, saith Jehovah.* Note the distinction made in the text differentiating this new covenant from the older one made when Israel was delivered from Egyptian captivity, which was later broken by the people with whom it was made. The following portion of the text is very revealing and informative: *For this is the covenant that I will make with the house of Israel, after those days, saith Jehovah:* Having initially identified the two houses, the prophecy now pinpoints a single and unified house of Israel as the party with whom this new covenant would be made. Bear in mind that the northern kingdom was called Israel while the southern kingdom was called Judah, and also that the northern kingdom had never again been reconstituted in any way or form since its conquest. Only Judah saw the resemblance of a reconstitution after it regained partial autonomy as a Babylonian province. The two separate kingdoms have never been reunited since their division till today. The clear deduction here is that the New Covenant is yet to be instituted because it is to be established with a unified Kingdom of Israel, which until now is yet to be restored. The futuristic nature of the Jeremiah 31 prophecy is thus demonstrated.

Regarding the erroneous Christian theology, as earlier noted, the alleged new covenant instituted by Jesus was not with the house of Israel but with few of his disciples in the province of Judah. This does not correspond with the details provided in the text, as recently noted (the renewal being made with a full and united Israel). Furthermore, the unique features of this new covenant, which distinguish it from the older covenant, are provided in the text thus: *I will put my law in their inward parts, and will write it in their heart; and I will be their God and they shall be my people. And they shall teach no more every man his neighbour, and every man his brother, saying, Know Jehovah; for they shall all know me, from the least of them unto the greatest of them, saith Jehovah: for I will pardon their iniquity, and their sin will I remember no more.* With the older covenant, the law was written on tablets of stone, but with the new covenant, it will be written inwardly in the hearts of the other covenanting party (Israel). A very crucial feature of the new covenant is that it would no longer be necessary teaching others the associated law because, having been written in the heart, everyone who partakes of the covenant would naturally know the law. This is what is coming once the covenant is eventually renewed, but it is not the case with what applies in Christianity under the supposed new covenant instituted by Jesus—where the law is not written in the heart, thus necessitating the need for it to be taught as often as possible. This aspect of the Christian new covenant again contradicts the provisions of the prophecy, thus revealing that it cannot rightly be regarded as the fulfilment of the prophecy.

The promised new covenant, therefore, is yet to be instituted and fulfilled but will be at the right time and with the right people; the people it was promised—Israel. The instituting of the New Covenant (or the renewal of the Covenant) is an integral part of the restoration of Israel.

As per the actual restoration process, Joel 1–2 gives an insight starting with a figurative description of the deplorable state of Israel in captivity before instructing on the needful and ending in the hope of salvation for all who would repent and call on the name of the Lord God of Israel, as recorded thus: *The word of Jehovah that came to Joel the son of Pethuel. Hear this, ye old*

men, and give ear, all ye inhabitants of the land. Hath this been
in your days, or even in the days of your fathers? Tell your
children of it, and let your children tell their children, and their
children another generation: that which the palmer-worm hath
left hath the locust eaten; and that which the locust hath left hath
the cankerworm eaten; and that which the cankerworm hath left
hath the caterpillar eaten. Awake, ye drunkards, and weep; and
howl, all ye drinkers of wine, because of the new wine: for it is cut
off from your mouth. For a nation is come up upon my land,
strong and without number: his teeth are the teeth of a lion, and
he hath the cheek teeth of a lioness. He hath made my vine a
desolation, and barked my fig-tree; he hath made it clean bare,
and cast it away: its branches are made white. Wail like a virgin
girded with sackcloth for the husband of her youth. The oblation
and the drink-offering are cut off from the house of Jehovah; the
priests, Jehovah's ministers, mourn. The field is laid waste, the
land mourneth; for the corn is wasted, the new wine is dried up,
the oil languisheth. Be ashamed, ye husbandmen; howl, ye
vinedressers, for the wheat and for the barley: because the harvest
of the field hath perished. The vine is dried up, and the fig-tree
languisheth; the pomegranate-tree, the palm also and the apple-
tree; all the trees of the field are withered, yea, joy is withered
away from the children of men. Gird yourselves, and lament, ye
priests; howl, ministers of the altar; come, lie all night in sackcloth, ye ministers of my God for the oblation and the
drink-offering are withholden from the house of your God.
Hallow a fast, proclaim a solemn assembly, gather the elders, and
all the inhabitants of the land to the house of Jehovah your God
and cry unto Jehovah. Alas for the day! for the day of Jehovah is
at hand, and as destruction from the Almighty shall it come. Is

not the food cut off before our eyes, joy and gladness from the house of our God The seeds are rotten under their clods, the granaries are laid desolate, the barns are broken down; for the corn is withered. How do the beasts groan! The herds of cattle are bewildered, for they have no pasture; the flocks of sheep also are in suffering. To thee, Jehovah, do I cry; for the fire hath devoured the pastures of the wilderness, and the flame hath burned up all the trees of the field. The beasts of the field also cry unto thee; for the water-courses are dried, and the fire hath devoured the pastures of the wilderness (Joel 1 DARBY).

Joel 2 now continues with the prophecy, starting with a clarion call detailing specific actions that need to be taken by Israel for their restoration: *Blow the trumpet in Zion, and sound an alarm in my holy mountain; let all the inhabitants of the land tremble: for the day of Jehovah cometh, for it is at hand; a day of darkness and gloom, a day of clouds and gross darkness, as the dawn spread upon the mountains; — a great people and a strong; there hath not been ever the like, neither shall be any more after them, to the years of generations and generations. A fire devoureth before them, and behind them a flame burneth; the land is as a garden of Eden before them, and behind them a desolate wilderness: yea, and nothing escapeth them. The appearance of them is as the appearance of horses; and as horsemen, so they run. Like the noise of chariots, on the tops of the mountains, they leap; like the noise of a flame of fire that devoureth the stubble, as a strong people set in battle array. Before them the peoples are in anguish: all faces turn pale. They run like mighty men; they climb the wall like men of war; and they march every one on his ways, and break not their ranks.*

Neither doth one press upon another; they march every one in his path; and fall amid weapons, but are not wounded. They spread themselves over the city; they run upon the wall; they climb up into the houses; they enter in by the windows like a thief. The earth quaketh before them; the heavens tremble; the sun and the moon are darkened, and the stars withdraw their shining. And Jehovah uttereth his voice before his army; for his camp is very great; for strong is he that executeth his word: for the day of Jehovah is great and very terrible; and who can bear it? Yet even now, saith Jehovah, turn to me with all your heart, and with fasting, and with weeping, and with mourning; and rend your heart, and not your garments, and turn unto Jehovah your God for he is gracious and merciful, slow to anger, and of great loving-kindness, and repenteth him of the evil. Who knoweth? He might return and repent, and leave a blessing behind him, an oblation and a drink-offering for Jehovah your God Blow the trumpet in Zion, hallow a fast, proclaim a solemn assembly; gather the people, hallow the congregation, assemble the elders, gather the children, and those that suck the breasts; let the bridegroom go forth from his chamber, and the bride from her closet. Let the priests, the ministers of Jehovah, weep between the porch and the altar, and let them say, Spare, O Jehovah, thy people, and give not thine inheritance to reproach, that they should be a byword of the nations. Wherefore should they say among the peoples, Where is their God Then Jehovah will be jealous for his land, and will have pity on his people. And Jehovah will answer and say unto his people, Behold, I send you corn, and new wine, and oil, and ye shall be satisfied therewith; and I will no more make you a reproach among the nations. And I will remove far off from you him that cometh from the north, and will drive him into a land barren and desolate, his face toward the eastern sea, and his rear toward the hinder sea; and his stench shall come up, and his ill odour shall come up, for he hath exalted himself to do great things. — Fear not, O land; be glad and rejoice: for Jehovah doeth great things. Be not afraid, ye beasts of the field: for the pastures of the wilderness do spring; for the tree beareth its fruit; the fig-tree and the vine yield full increase. And ye, children of Zion, be glad and rejoice in Jehovah your God for he giveth you the early rain in due measure, and he causeth to come down for you the rain, the early rain, and the latter rain at the beginning of the season. And the floors shall be full of corn, and the vats shall overflow with new wine and oil. And I will restore to you the years that the locust hath eaten, the cankerworm, and the caterpillar, and the palmer-worm, my great army which I sent among you. And ye shall eat in plenty, and be satisfied, and praise the name of Jehovah your God who hath dealt wondrously with you: and my people shall never be ashamed. And ye shall know that I am in the midst of Israel, and that I, Jehovah, am your God and there is none else: and my people shall never be ashamed. And it shall come to pass afterwards that I will pour out my Spirit upon all flesh; and your sons and your daughters shall prophesy, your old men shall dream dreams, your young men shall see visions. Yea, even upon the bondmen and upon the handmaids in those days will I pour out my Spirit. And I will shew wonders in the heavens and on the earth, blood, and fire, and pillars of smoke. The sun shall be changed to darkness, and the moon to blood, before the great and terrible day of Jehovah come. 32And it shall be that whosoever shall call upon the name of Jehovah shall be saved: for in mount Zion and in Jerusalem shall be deliverance, as Jehovah hath said, and for the residue whom Jehovah shall call (Joel 2 DARBY).

The referenced text needs no further commentary because it is well detailed and self-explanatory. Instead, we shall next consider these reasonable questions: When will the prophecy be fulfilled? How will this fulfilment pan out? For answers, historical precedence is again invaluable.

The first historical restoration occurred when Israel was delivered from Egyptian captivity, thus beginning their journey into nationhood. With respect to the timing of this earlier restoration, this happened after the completion of the four hundred years stipulated by God to Abraham, as noted previously. As per the how, God appointed a leader; Moses, through whom instructions and guidelines were provided for every step of the journey from Egypt to Canaan. The Book of Exodus provides ample details about the deliverance of Israel from Egyptian captivity—including the deplorable state of the Israelites in Egypt at the time, the call of Moses, his confrontation and negotiation with Pharaoh, the Exodus, journey through the wilderness, and the instituting of the first covenant (the old).

Another historical restoration relates to the partial reconstitution of Judah in line with Jeremiah's prophecy, as noted previously. In this case, the timing of the restoration was based on the associated prophecy (seventy years), while the how was also based on God's guidance. The restoration took place after the seventy years stipulated in Jeremiah's prophecy: In 516 BC, exactly seventy years from the Babylonian conquest of Jerusalem in 586 BC. Regarding the actual restoration process (the How), God again appointed a number of people, each of whom performed various responsibilities culminating in the eventual restoration. The list includes the following people: Daniel—who took it upon himself to fast and pray for the fulfilment of the prophecy (Daniel 9), Nehemiah—who played a leading role in the rebuilding of Jerusalem and her walls (Nehemiah 1–7), and Ezra—who presided over the instructing of the people in the law of the Lord (Nehemiah 8–10).

What is immediately evident is that God, who made the promise of restoration, also knows the when and how of this second and final restoration of Israel. Does that then preclude the people themselves from any responsibility or action? No. Both the earlier deliverance from Egyptian captivity and the later restoration of Judah all required active participation on the part of the Israelites. Similarly, this final restoration of Israel will require the active involvement of the people who are to be restored.

The Awakening

The restoration process cannot start until the people to be restored are aware of their true identity, their need for restoration, and that their restoration was promised. So, the first event to kick-start the fulfilment of the prophecies about the final restoration of Israel would be the rediscovering of their rightful identity by today's true descendants of the Israelites. I believe this will come through a gradual awakening, starting with a few individuals (the harbingers), before culminating in a mass awareness through which all Israelites today (or at the time) would be awakened to their true identity. Current events suggest that the initial stage of this awakening has already started; some Black Africans are beginning to come to the awareness of their

Hebrew origins, especially those in the US, UK and some African countries like Nigeria and Ghana. This awakening is represented in the recent proliferation within the Hebrew Roots Movement, where more and more Black Africans in parts of the world are now recognising their true heritage, including their Hebraic roots, particularly Israelite ancestry.

Personally, I came to this awakening in 2015 through a series of supernatural encounters and revelations. Since then, I have come across a significant number of people who had also experienced a similar awakening. Noting here that this awakening can only be experienced through a revelation from God will suffice. Other than that, I cannot confidently provide any further details in this regard. Consequently, instead of trying to forcefully "awaken" other Israelites, as seems to be the case in some quarters, those Israelites who have already experienced this awakening should pray for the other Israelites to also come to a similar awakening as themselves. More so, those Israelites who are now aware of their true heritage should also earnestly seek God for revelation regarding the roles and responsibilities appointed for them in this final restoration, including how to assist those other modern-day Israelites who are still ignorant or sceptical about who they truly are.

It is very important to clarify here, based on my opinion, that not every current Black African is an Israelite, even if truly of Hebrew origin. Hebrews, as previously noted, include every descendant of Abraham, including those who are descended through Ishmael, Esau, and the other six sons born through Keturah from whom many nations arose. The keyword in this restoration therefore is Israel, because the prophecy is specifically unto Israel, and not Hebrew.

Religion is another very important factor related to this restoration. As noted, Judaism, Christianity, and Islam; three of the world's major religions common among the general population within which today's descendants of Israelites are believed to be mainly assimilated, all present a serious challenge in this regard because each of these religions upholds core beliefs which are opposed to the identity, heritage, and future of the ethnic Israelites. With Judaism, the practitioners (Jews) claim to be the heirs of the promise. In Islam, the descendants of Ishmael are believed to be the true heirs of the promise. While in Christianity, the Church (representing Christians) is the new or spiritual Israel. Proving the rightness or wrongness of these claims is not the objective here and so would not be necessary.

However, it is very important to highlight them because any true Israelite who is caught up in such erroneous beliefs faces difficulty in realising their true identity. Such beliefs pose a serious obstacle to the rediscovering of a person's true identity as an Israelite. With Christianity in particular, an Israelite practitioner or believer, instead of expecting the fulfilment of the prophecy about the restoration of Israel, is taught to expect the return of Jesus Christ. And because religious belief is a very strong force, such belief would stand in strong opposition against the acceptance of the truth even when God, through the Spirit attempts to make this revelation to a person. Be that as it may, God is greater and stronger than any forces of deception and is able against all odds to break through religious strongholds and liberate captives.

The awakening, in any case, has already began and will expand, culminating in the global awakening during which all modern-day Israelites will all dawn on their true identity regardless of what identity they had previously presumed or currently hold on to. Whatever God says stands. God's word never fails, and whatever God has promised, He always performs. Israel will again be restored. In God's own time and in accordance with God's plans. Arise! O, Israel.

Afterword

Who are the Israelites, and what is Israel? We shall start with the second question. Israel is more than just a country, nation-state, or political entity. Israel represents God's intention for a model kingdom through which His plans for the whole world would be revealed. Attesting to this is the fact that Israel is the only kingdom in the entire world whose leader or king was chosen by God; starting from Moses, Israel's first leader, through Solomon, the last king to rule over a united Israel. It is instructive to note that God's plan for the world through Israel did not initially pan out before Israel was subsequently conquered and destroyed, mainly because of the various failures of the Israelites themselves. The plan was hinged on the Abrahamic Covenant, which required the Israelites to abide by the requirements integral to the covenant. Israel was chosen and blessed by God to be a blessing to the entire world, by standing as a beacon of light and hope through whom the rest of the world would witness the love of God. The expectation was that God's blessings over Israel as they trusted and obeyed Him would inspire the other nations of the world to emulate Israel's example by turning to the God of Israel,

Elohim, and away from their various gods in their idolatry. But Israel failed, because of the people, although the plan still stands. Hence the plan for the final restoration of Israel. Note here that God alone decides what Israel is because Israel was God's idea in the first place. Therefore, as it was with the initial constituting, the later reconstituting of Israel will be down to God and not any worldly institutions (e.g., the UN). It is God who will announce Israel to the world and not a human or institution.

Now to the first question about who the Israelites are. The children of Israel, as they are commonly referred to, descended from Jacob, who was the second son of Isaac who was also the second son of Abraham (but the child God promised Abraham). The other descendants of Abraham through Ishmael (Abraham's first son born by a maid), Esau (Isaac's first son), and the other six sons born to Abraham by Keturah, his second wife (married after the demise of Abraham's first wife Sarah), although all rightly Hebrew, are not Israelites. The history of the Israelites is well accounted for in the Hebrew Bible; Israelites are the main subject of the Hebrew Bible. Israel's historiography reveals that the people were conquered and expelled from their land. It is instructive to note that these Israelites were never made extinct, through annihilation, but rather were scattered across different parts of the world where they would eventually be absorbed and assimilated into the cultures of their various host communities. So the Israelites continue to exist today, howbeit under different ethnic identities. Biblical and other secular historical records reveal Africa as the main continent where the ancient Israelites fled to—this includes places now under today's Middle East. From Africa some of these Israelite descendants would subsequently be scattered to more parts of the world. History reveals that Transatlantic Slavery took some of them from Africa to other continents, notable Europe, and North and South America. Other forms of migration in successive periods resulted in some among them travelling to almost every corner of the world.

It is important to note that the Israelites were originally dark-skinned (or today's black).

In addition to their ethnic identity, is the spiritual identity of the Israelites; they are the people chosen by God, just as Israel is a kingdom chosen by God, as a role model representing God's plan for humanity at large. The Israelites were chosen to represent God's righteousness among humans so that through them, the rest of humanity would be inspired to also live righteously. A greater part of this righteousness or way of living is embodied in the Abrahamic Covenant. But the Israelites failed. Instead of living by the covenant, they regularly deviated into idolatry. Ironically, instead of inspiring the people of the other nations (Gentiles) into turning to their God, as was the plan, the Israelites allowed themselves to be influenced by their neighbouring gentile nations into idolatry. Hence they were conquered by these other nations and subsequently scattered across the world. But all hope is not lost.

The Israelites, as Israel, will be restored, and this time for good because it will be an eternal restoration. Primarily, because the covenant associated with this restoration will be significantly different to that associated with the initial constituting of Israel; instead of on tablets of stone, the law will be put in the inward parts of the people. This will ensure both a perfect understanding of the law as well as full compliance with its requirements. Again, God decides who is an Israelite, and not humans or institutions, because it was God who chose them in the first place. God will also announce the Israelites to the world once their final restoration is accomplished.

Israel and the Israelites are, therefore, pivotal in God's plan for the world. Perhaps the role the Israelites play in God's plan for the world is the main reason behind their plights. Apart from being expelled from their land, the Israelites would eventually also lose their identity in exchange for various false identities occasioned by their assimilation into other ethnic cultures and global communities. Hence they are believed to be lost—historically. This loss of identity is perhaps the biggest of all the misfortunes which have befallen the Israelites since they became a people, some of which are still ongoing. This is underlined by the fact that regaining their true and original identity is a key prerequisite for their restoration: Until the Israelites realise who they truly are, it would be difficult for them to play their role in their final restoration. While God will play a major role in both the regaining of their true identity and their restoration, the Israelites themselves are not exempt from taking any actions. For instance, while God will inspire and stir their awakening, it is up to the Israelites to acknowledge this and to act accordingly.

The primary reason I have written this book is to inspire and stir this awakening among every of today's Israelites, as I have been inspired and guided by the God of Israel, Elohim, the Most High.

All thanks and praises be to The Most High!

List of Illustrations

7. Fig 3c. Historical map of old Americas. The New York Public Library",
    https://digitalcollections.nypl.org/items/510d47db-b1fa-a3d9-
    e040e00a18064a99

8. Fig 3d. Historical map of old Eurasia and Australasia.
    https://www.mapsland.com/asia/old-maps-of-asia/large-detaile-old-
    antique-political-map-of-asia-1743

9. Fig 4a. The partition of Africa during colonisation. Ro Ho.
    Published on November 18, 2012. https://originalpeople.org/scramble-
    for-africa-par/

10. Fig 4b. Map showing the biblical boundaries of Israel.
    https://theisraelbible.com/2016/04/07/biblical-boundaries-land-israel

11. Fig 5a. Albinism. BBC. https://www.bbc.co.uk/news/health-
    10697682

12. Fig 5b. Albinism: Black mother with white children. The Mirror.
    https://www.mirror.co.uk/news/uk-news/black-mum-and-dad-have-
    three-white-416455

13. Fig 5c. Albinism. Black parents a white child. New York Post.
    https://nypost.com/2010/07/21/blond-bombshell

14. Fig.6a Black American-Indians. https://www.blackhis-
    tory.com/2019/11/first-americans-were-black-indians-african-de-
    scent.html

15. Fig 6b. Black Europe: Black people in renaissance Europe. Museo
    Nacional   del   Prado,   Madrid.   https://www.ny-
    times.com/2012/11/09/arts/design/african-presence-in-renaissance-
    europe-at-walters-museum.html

16. Fig 6c. Black Europe: Moorish kings and queens in Europe.
    https://www.blackhistory.com/2019/08/moors-black-kings-queens-
    ruled-europe-almost-700-years.html

17. Fig 7a. An Oba of ancient Benin Kingdom. Giulio Ferrario. IL Costume Antico & Moderno (Milano, 1815-1827), vol. https://commons.wiki-media.org/wiki/File:Oba_of_Benin_1600s.jpg

18. Fig 8a. Captives on board a ship on the West Coast of Africa c.1880. Ann Ronan Pictures/Getty Images.

19. Fig 8b. Diagram of the "Brookes" slave ship. Thomas Clarkson. The British Library.

20. Fig 9. List of Black inventors and inventions. Natasha Abdullah. https://www.pinterest.co.uk/pin/AQck0_y3VmtUxeV-KsGIxAFMwx8CwO72EPi_6igXqgeo0Egf61_l6cJc/

21. Fig 10. Timeline of the biblical history of Israel. Microsoft Bing, Bing Images. https://www.pinterest.co.uk/pin/548242954617823360/

Bibliography

1. *The Holy Bible.* YouVersion
2. John F. Hoffecker. *Modern Humans: Their African Origin And Global Dispersal.* Columbia University Press. 2017
3. James Owen. *Modern Humans Came Out of Africa, "Definitive" Study Says.* news.nationalgeographic.com. 18 July 2007
4. Ethan Bronner. *Inventing the Notion of Race; Some Scholars Say the Label Evolved Recently, As a Tool of the Vanquished as Well as the Victors.* nytimes.com. 1998
5. Elizabeth Kolbert. *There's No Scientific Basis for Race — It's a Made-Up Label.* nationalgeographic.com. (undated)
6. *Research confirms theory that all modern humans descended from the same small group of people.* phys.org. 8 May 2007
7. Donald Johanson. *Origin of Modern Humans* actionbioscience.org. May 2001
8. David Derbyshire. *Is this how Eve spoke? Every language evolved from 'single prehistoric African mother tongue'.*

dailymail.co.uk. 15 April 17 2011 (updated 17 April 2011)

9. Ann Gibbons. *How Europeans evolved white skin.* sciencemag.org. 2 April 2015

10. Genographic Project. *Map of Human Migration.* nationalgeographic.com. (undated)

11. Connie J. Kolman, Nyamkhishig Sambuughin and Eldredge Bermingham. *Mitochondrial DNA Analysis of Mongolian Populations and Implications for the Origin of New World Founders.* GENETICS. April 1, 1996 vol. 142 no. 4 1321-1334

12. Paul Rincon. *Cheddar Man: DNA shows early Briton had dark skin.* bbc.co.uk. 23 February 2018

13. Tamm E, Kivisild T, Reidla M, Metspalu M, Smith DG, Mulligan CJ, et al. *Beringian Standstill and Spread of Native American Founders* PLoS ONE 2(9): e829. 2007 (doi: 10.1371/journal.pone.0000829)

14. Connie J. Kolman, Nyamkhishig Sambuughin and Eldredge Bermingham. *Mitochondrial DNA Analysis of Mongolian Populations and Implications for the Origin of New World Founders.* GENETICS. April 1, 1996 vol. 142 no. 4 1321-1334

15. Maanasa Raghavan, Matthias Steinrucken, Rasmus Nielsen, et al. *Genomic evidence for the Pleistocene and recent population history of Native Americans.* SCIENCE. 21 August 2015 vol. 349, Issue 6250, aab3884 (doi: 10.1126/science.aab3884)

16. Pontus Skoglund, Swapan Mallick, et al. *Genetic evidence for two founding populations of the Americas.* NATURE 525,104-108. 03 September 2015

17. Noreen von Cramon-Taubadel, Andre Strauss, et al. *Evolutionary population history of early Paleoamerican cranial morphology.* SCIENCE ADVANCES. 22 February 2017: vol. 3, no. 2, e1602289 (doi: 10. 1126/sciadv. 1602289)

18. Morten Rasmussen, Sarah L. Anzick, et al. *The genome of a Late Pleistocene human from a Clovis burial site in western Montana.* NATURE 506, 225-229. 13 February 2014

19. Bourgeon L, Burke A, Higham T. *Earliest Human Presence in North America Dated to the Last Glacial Maximum: New Radiocarbon Dates from Bluefish Caves, Canada.* PLoS ONE 12(1): e0169486 (doi: 10. 1371/journal.pone.0169486). 2017

20. Dillehay TD, Ocampo C, Saavedra J, Sawakuchi AO, Vega RM, Pino M, et al. *New Archaeological Evidence for an Early Human Presence at Monte Verde, Chile.* PLoS ONE 10(11): e0141923 (doi: 10. 1371/journal.pone.0141923). 2015

21. Hogenboom Melissa. *The first people who populated the Americas.* bbc.com. 30 March 2017

22. BBC Documentary series. *Ancient Voices: The hunt for the first Americans.* BBC Two. 1 September 1999 2130 BST

23. BBC News online. *'First Americans were Australia'.* bbc.co.uk. 26 August 1999

24. Oliver, Douglas L. *Oceania: The Native Cultures of Australia and the Pacific Islands.* University of Hawaii Press. 1989

25. Fran Dorey. *The First Modern Humans in Southeast Asia*. australianmuseum.net.au. 04 January 2010

26. The Columbia Encyclopedia, 6th edition. *Dravidians* encyclopedia.com. 06 September 2018

27. Michael Loewe, Edward L. Shaughnessy. *The Cambridge History of Ancient China: From the Origins of Civilization to 221 BC.* Cambridge University Press. 1999

28. Sobecki Sebastian. *New World Discovery.* oxford handbooks.com. November 2015 (doi: 10. 1093/oxfordhb/ 9780199935338.013.141)

29. Donald Weinstein, Judith Eleanor Herrin et al. *History of Europe: The Germans and Huns.* Encyclopaedia Britannica. November 26, 2020

30. The New York Times. *Civilization Owes Debt to an African Egypt.* December 10, 1989, Section 4, Page 22

31. Mungo Park. *Travels in the Interior of Africa.* 1799

32. The Oriental Institute. *The History of Ancient Nubia.* The University of Chicago Online

33. US Library of Congress. *The Earliest South Africans*

34. National Geographic Online. *Africa: Human Geography*

35. Ajayi J.F. Ade and Crowder Michael. *History of West Africa.* Longman. 1985

36. Ham Anthony. *West Africa.* Lonely Planet. 2009

37. Jacques Gernet. *A history of Chinese civilization.* Cambridge University Press. 1996

38. Mark Edward Lewis. *China's cosmopolitan empire: The Tang dynasty.* Harvard University Press. 2009

39. Chancellor Williams. *The Destruction of Black Civilization: Great Issues of A Race from 4500BC to 2000AD.* Third World Press. 1994

40. Djibril Tamsir Niane, Editor. *General History of Africa IV: Africa from the Twelfth to the Sixteenth Century.* UNESCO. 1984

41. George T. Stride and Caroline Ifeka. *Peoples and Empires of West Africa; West Africa in History, 1000-1800.* Holmes and Meier Publishers. 1971

42. Robert O. Collins and James M. Burns. *A History of Sub-Saharan Africa.* Cambridge University Press. 2007

43. Christopher Ehret. *The Civilizations of Africa.* University of Virginia. 2002

44. John Iliffe. *Africans: The History of a Continent* (Second edition). Cambridge University Press. 2007

45. Keith Lye. *Encyclopedia of African Nations and Civilization.* The Diagram Group. 2002

46. Phyllis M. Martin, Patrick O'Meara. *Africa* (Third edition). Indiana University Press. 1995

47. Willie F. Page. *Encyclopedia of African History and Culture: From Conquest to Colonization (1500-1850).* Learning Source Books. 2001

48. Kevin Shillington. *History of Africa* (Revised second edition). Palgrave Macmillan. 2005

49. Hugh Chisholm, Editor. *'Africa'* Encyclopaedia Britannica (Eleventh edition). Cambridge University Press. 1911

50. Nicolas Grimal. *A History of Ancient Egypt.* Basilblackwell. 1992

51. Peter Fryer. *Staying Power: The History of Black People in Britain.* PlutoPress. 1984

52. David Olusoga. *Black and British: A Forgotten History.* Panmacmillan. 2016

53. The Editors of Encyclopaedia Britannica. *Hebrew.* Encyclopaedia Britannica. April 17, 2019

54. Andre Parrot. *Abraham.* Encyclopaedia Britannica. March 24, 2020

55. James A. Montgomery. *Arabia and the Bible.* University of Philadelphia Press. 1934 (Reprint 2016 ed.)

56. Frederick Victor Winnett, William LaForest Reed. *Ancient Records from North Arabia.* University of Toronto Press. 1970

57. The Editors of Encyclopaedia Britannica. *Canaan.* Encyclopaedia Britannica. October 11, 2019

58. The Editors of Encyclopaedia Britannica. *Exodus.* Encyclopaedia Britannica. January 14, 2020

59. Kristin Romey. *Living Descendants of Biblical Canaanites Identified Via DNA.* Nationalgeographic.com. 2017

60. Marc Haber, Claude Doumet-Serhal, et al. *Continuity and Admixture in the Last Five Millennia of Levantine History from Ancient Canaanite and Present-Day Lebanese Genome Sequences.* American Journal of Human Genetics cell.com (doi: doi.org/10.1016/j.ajhg.2017.06.013). 2017

61. Flavius Josephus. *Antiquities of the Jews Book 1*

62. The History of Herodotus. *Herodotus Book 4: Melpomene [170]* sacred-texts.com

63. The History of Herodotus. *Herodotus Book 2: Euterpe [50]* sacred-texts.com

64. Hemingway Sean and Colette Hemingway. *Africans in Ancient Greek Art.* In Heilbrunn Timeline of Art History, New York: The Metropolitan Museum of Art. met museum.org. 2008

65. Redfern RC, Grocke D, Millard AR, Ridgeway V, Johnson L. *Going south of the river: A multidisciplinary analysis of ancestry, mobility and diet in a population from Roman Southwark, London.* Journal of Archaeological Science 2016 74 11-22.

66. Rebecca C Redfern, Michael Marshall, Katherine Eaton, Hendrik Poinar. *'Written in Bone': New discoveries about the Lives and Burials of Four Roman Londoners.* Britannia 48 (2017) 253-277 (doi: 10.1017/S0068113X17000216). 2017

67. Leach S, Eckardt H, Chenery C, Müldner G, Lewis M. (2010) *A lady of York: migration, ethnicity and identity in Roman York.* Antiquity 2010 84 131-135. 2010

68. Miranda Kaufmann. *Black Tudors: The Untold Story.* Oneworld Publications. 2017

69. Samuel Eliot Morison. *Journals and Other Documents on the Life and Voyages of Christopher Columbus.* Heritage Press. 1963

70. Leo Wiener. *Africa and the Discovery of America.* Innes and Sons. 1922

71. Joan Baxter. *Africa's 'greatest explorer'.* BBC News Online bbc.co.uk. 2000

72. Martin Bernal. *Black Athena: The Afroasiatic Roots of Classical Civilization Volume One.* Vintage. 1991

73. Martin Bernal. *Black Athena: The Afroasiatic Roots of Classical Civilization Volume Two.* Rutgers University Press. 1991

74. Akan Takruri. *Africa's History & Migration: 200,000bc-3,000bc.* Lulu. 2017

75. Ryan Ellsworth. *Oldowan and Acheulean Stone Tools.* Museum of Anthropology, University of Missouri anthro-museum.missouri.edu. 2008

76. Adam Hart-Davis, editor. *History: The Definitive Visual Guide - From the Dawn of Civilization to the Present Day.* Dorling Kindersley Publishing. 2012

77. Kathryn A. Bard. *The Emergence of the Egyptian State (c. 3200 - 2686 BC). In The Oxford History of Ancient Egypt* (Ian Shaw, editor) Oxford University Press. 2000

78. James M. McPherson. *The Abolitionist Legacy: From Reconstruction to the NAACP.* Princeton University Press. 1995

79. Junius P Rodriguez. *The Historical Encyclopedia of World Slavery, Vol 1; Vol 7.* ABC-CLIO. 1997

80. Milton Meltzer. *Slavery: A World History.* Da Capo Press. 1993

81. Olaudah Equiano. *The Interesting Narrative of the Life of Olaudah Equiano, Or Gustavus Vassa, The African.* Olaudah Equiano (self-published). 1789

82. Paul Finkelman, Cary D. Wintz. *Encyclopedia of African American History, 1896 to the Present: From the Age of Segregation to the Twenty-first Century* (Five-volume Set). Oxford University Press. 2009

83. Roger B. Beck. *The History of South Africa.* Greenwood Publishing Group. 2000

84. Keith Kyle. *The Politics of the Independence of Kenya* Macmillan. 1999

85. Audie Klotz. *Norms in International Relations: The Struggle Against Apartheid.* Cornell University Press. 1999

86. Charles E. Cobb Jr. *No Easy Victories: African Liberation and American Activists Over a Half Century, 1950–2000.* William Minter. 2008

87. Robin Hallet. *Africa to 1875: A Modern History.* University of Michigan Press. 1970

88. Robin Hallet. *Africa Since 1875: A Modern History.* Diane Publishing Company. 1974

89. Sophie Morlin-Yron. *What's the real size of Africa? How Western states used maps to downplay size of continent.* CNN World (March 23, 2017) cnn.com. 2017

90. Melinda D. Anderson. *What Kids Are Really Learning About Slavery.* The Atlantic. theAtlantic.com. 2018

91. Colin Kidd. *The Forging of Races: Race and Scripture in the Protestant Atlantic World, 1600-2000.* Cambridge University Press. 2006

92. Robert Lensink. *Structural Adjustment in sub-Saharan Africa.* Longman. 1996

93. The Sentencing Project. *Report to the United Nations on Racial Disparities in the U.S. Criminal Justice System.* sentencing project.org. April 2018

94. Carol Lancaster. *Africa's Economic Crisis.* Foreign Policy No. 52 (Autumn, 1983), pp. 149-166 (doi: 10.2307/1148240) jstor.org. 1983

95. Mark Langan. *Neo-Colonialism and the Poverty of 'Development' in Africa.* Palgrave Macmillan. 2017

96. Walter Rodney. *How Europe Underdeveloped Africa.* Pambazuka Press. 2012

97. Thomas Pakenham. *The Scramble for Africa: White Man's Conquest of the Dark Continent from 1876 to 1912.* Avon Books. 1992

98. Hugh Seton-Watson. *The New Imperialism.* Dufour. 1962

99. Kevin Shillington. *History of Africa.* Revised second edition. Macmillan Education. 1995

100. Michelle Alexander. *The New Jim Crow: Mass Incarceration in the Age of Colorblindness.* The New Press. 2010